# The Rev.
# Samuel Harrison

Abolitionist, Activist, and Chaplain of the
Massachusetts 54th, the First Black Regiment
Raised in the North to Fight in the Civil War

Ann-Elizabeth Barnes

Crow Flies Press
The Berkshires, Massachusetts

# Timeline for Events Leading to the Civil War

| Year | Event |
|------|-------|
| 1613 | Jan Rodrigues, an African left behind by a Dutch sailing vessel, settles in Manhattan, first non-native resident of America |
| 1619 | First cargo of kidnapped and enslaved Africans arrives at the English colony of Jamestown, VA |
| 1620 | Pilgrims arrive at Plimouth Rock |
| 1638 | First documented enslaved Africans arrive in Boston |
| 1701 | First documented court case of a slave suing successfully for his freedom in Massachusetts |
| 1724 | First settlers arrive in Sheffield |
| 1744 | Elizabeth "Mumbet" Freeman born around this date in New York State |
| 1746 | First documented free blacks in Stockbridge, Cuffee and Nana Negro, manumitted by their owner, Elias Van Schaack |
| 1759 | Agrippa Hull born to free Black parents in Northampton, MA. Comes to Stockbridge while still a child a few years later |
| 1773 | Sheffield Declaration written in Sheffield, "all men are free, equal and independent of each other" |
| 1770 | Boston Massacre, first man to die for the cause of independence, Crispus Attucks, free Black living in Boston |
| 1776 | Declaration of Independence is written "all men are created free and equal" |
| 1780 | Massachusetts Constitution is ratified using same language "all men are free and equal" |
| 1781 | Elizabeth "Mumbet" Freeman successfully sues for her freedom, based on new Constitution, setting stage for abolition of slavery in MA |
| 1783 | Massachusetts bans slavery by judicial decree (Supreme Court Judge Cushing) |
| 1783 | September--end of the American Revolution |
| 1787 | Shay's Rebellion, returning Massachetts soldiers successfully protest unfair taxation and seizure of property in "last battle of the war." |

1787  U.S. Constitution ratified, includes clause counting slaves as 3/5 of a person for calculating each States' population, benefiting South

1789  Olaudah Equiano, kidnapped from Africa at age 11, escapes slavery, and writes autobiography about horrors of slavery

1793  US Congress passes first "Fugitive Slave Law" making it illegal to hide runaway slaves

1802  Rebellion in Haiti forces France to end the slave trade

1807  Britain ends the slave trade

1808  Congress prohibits the importation of slaves, ends the slave trade

1818  Samual Harrison born in Philadelphia on April 15th to enslaved parents

1820  Missouri Compromise: in conjunction with the admission of Maine as a free state, Missouri is allowed to organize as a slave state. But any new state thereafter, north of the Louisiana Purchase, will be organized as a free state.

1827  New York State abolishes slavery

1830  Abolitionists begin more thoroughly organizing the Underground Railroad, a series of safe houses ~ 10 miles apart, a secret network of individuals, both Black, White, free & enslaved, who helped slaves find their way north to freedom. Onus on slaves to find their way.

1834  Slavery abolished in the British Empire

1845  Frederick Douglass, former slave, publishes his first autobiography

1839  Successful revolt on the Spanish slave ship Amistad

1848  Connecticut abolishes slavery

1850  Compromise of 1850 --"popular sovereignty" let the people decide whether to be free or slave states. Congress has no right to impose decision. Guts Missouri Compromise

1850  Congress passes the Second Fugitive Slave Act, in response to Compromise of 1850, giving slave owners right to pursue runaway slaves in free states,

& requiring states to return slaves, making it illegal
to harbor them

1850    Harriet Tubman begins aiding slaves to escape the South
via the Underground Railroad.

1853    Harriet Beecher Stowe publishes "Uncle Tom's Cabin" to
great acclaim. Millions read it and are turned against
slavery

1854    Kansas-Nebraska Act, excercising "free sovereignty" law
(right of state to choose to be free or slave-owning):
spawns riots, rebellions, abolitionist John Brown raids
Pottawatimie Creek, in the end 200 dead, $2 million in
property damage.

1857    Dred Scott (a slave suing for his freedom) case: Supreme
Court decrees Blacks are not citizens therefore can be
considered property & it is unconstitutional to deprive an
individual of their property without due process of law.
(Uses Bill of Rights Fifth Amendment to deny Blacks
human rights, thin edge of wedge of war)

1857    West is expanding. New states coming in to existence.
Continuous angry debate about how to settle West: free or
enslaved. Dred Scott case makes it a constitutional issue
 that cannot be ignored much longer

1859    John Brown, abolitionist, raids Harper's Ferry for weapons
to arm a slave insurrection, captures federal arsenal, many
die. Robert E. Lee army takes it back. John Brown hanged.
South realizes it will have to secede from the Union to
protect itself and its right to own slaves.

1861    Civil War breaks out April 12. Lasts 4 years. Over 750,000
dead, many more maimed, wounded, impoverished.

1861    Congress takes steps to retract Fugitive Slave laws, making
it unlawful for anyone to return escaped or captured
slaves during war

1861-   Confederate (South) troops win most battles. Union
1862    morale low. War still claims to be about States rights to
govern themselves.

1862    Sept 17- Battle of Antietam, Union army wins at great
cost

1862    July, Congress passes Confiscation Act which frees

slaves living in Rebellion States & Militia Act so
Blacks can fight for Union v. South

1863  January 1st Lincoln reads the "Emancipation
      Proclamation" freeing all slaves.

1863  February, begin mustering men for the
      54th Massachusetts Volunteer Regiment first all Black
      Regiment raised in North, under Col. Robert Gould Shaw
      and spearheaded by Massachusetts Gov. John Andrew

1863  May 28th 54th and 55th Massachusetts Volunteer
      Regiments leave for South Carolina under
      Col. Robert Gould Shaw

1863  July 1-3-Battle of Gettysburg turning point of war gives
      Lincoln courage to make war about freeing all slaves

1863  July 18- Storming of Fort Wagner, Morris Island,
      Charleston Harbor, South Carolina by the
      54th Massachusetts Volunteer Regiment.
      Col. Shaw killed, buried with his men in unmarked
      grave.

1863  July-- Rev. Samuel Harrison visits the 54th Regiment
      in South Carolina on a mission of comfort.

1863  November-- Rev. Harrison musters into the army as
      Chaplain of the 54th. Offered half pay despite promises
      of equal pay. Begins protesting assisted by Gov. Andrew

1864  Thirteenth Amendment, outlawing slavery, passes
      Senate April 8th

1864  July, Harrison obtains equal pay for all Black soldiers
      with the help of Gov. Andrew and others

1865  April 9-- Robert E. Lee, Confederate General,
      surrenders to Ulysses S. Grant, Union General, at
      Appomattox Court House in Virginia

1865  April 14-- Abraham Lincoln shot by John Wilkes Booth,
      a maniacal actor. Andrew Johnson becomes president

1865  Reconstruction begins. Hopes are high for creating a
      place for all free Americans of African descent on
      U.S. soil.

1865  Pres. Andrew Johnson, a Southerner, mishandles
      Reconstruction, prolonging suffering of freed slaves,
      breeding a virulent form of racism that becomes as

great a curse as slavery. Reconstruction lasts until 1877 when North loses interest and the South institutes Jim Crow laws.

1865   Thirteenth Amendment, outlawing slavery, passes House January 31st

1865   Thirteenth Amendment, outlawing slavery, ratified December 6th (11 months later)

1866   Fourteenth Amendment ratified-granting citizenship and right to vote to people of African descent

1866   Fifteenth Amendment ratified--prohibiting States from denying vote to any man on the basis of "race, color or previous condition of servitude".

1868   William Edward Burghardt (W.E.B.) Du Bois born on February 24th in Great Barrington, MA

1877   End of "Reconstruction" beginning of Jim Crow era

1886   James VanderZee, Harlem Renaissance photographer, born in Lenox, MA.

1900   Samuel Harrison dies in Pittsfield, MA survived by two of his thirteen children.

*Broadside used to recruit Black soldiers with the promise of equal pay ($13/month) and a $100 bounty upon completion of their service*

Published by Crow Flies Press


The Rev. Samuel Harrison
Abolitionist, Activist, and Chaplain of the
Massachusetts 54th, the First Black Regiment Raised
in the North to Fight in the Civil War

ISBN 978-0-9983139-0-0

Library of Congress Control Number: 2016959836

Printed in the United States


Visit us on the Web! www.crowfliespress.com

# The Rev. Samuel Harrison

Abolitionist, Activist, and Chaplain of the
Massachusetts 54th, the First Black Regiment
Raised in the North to Fight in the Civil War

## Ann-Elizabeth Barnes

Crow Flies Press
The Berkshires, Massachusetts

.

Also by

Ann-Elizabeth Barnes

co-author of *"A Free Woman On God's Earth"*

*the True Story of Elizabeth "Mumbet" Freeman,*

*the Slave Who Won Her Freedom*

this book is dedicated to the

**Black Lives Matter**

**Movement**

and to all the men, women and children
who have been killed only
because of the color of their skin.

And to the idea of social justice and the
possibility of change

1899.

The Reverend Samuel Harrison, 1899

# The Rev.
# Samuel Harrison

Abolitionist, Activist, and Chaplain of the
Massachusetts 54th, the First Black Regiment
Raised in the North to Fight in the Civil War

Ann-Elizabeth Barnes

# Introduction

When I began writing this book I knew just the basics about the Civil War: that it was a war between the North and the South and that it was to abolish slavery. As I immersed myself in history books and the lore and stories of the time, and novels, my perspective was molded by a more modern interpretation of history and the role African Americans played in the development of America. And those readings did much to set the tone for this story.

In high school when learning about American history I often wondered why certain people supported Britain during the Revolutionary War and why others didn't. I don't remember it being emphasized that different races and nationalities made up the population of colonists during the early years of colonization. There were of course a melting pot of people then, including Irish, Scots, Welsh, French, Dutch, Belgian, Spanish, Africans, who all had their own particular gripe with the English. And that is why there was such diversity of reactions to the idea of a revolution against English rule.

I cannot recommend highly enough the works of Alan Taylor (Professor of History at UC Davis) and his 2001 book *American Colonies, the Settling of North America*. He has a brilliant ability to make something so complex seem simple and obvious. If I may quote from his introduction:

"To write a history of colonial America used to be easier, because the human cast and geographic stage were both considered so much smaller. Until the 1960's, most American historians assumed that "the colonists" meant English-speaking men confined to the Atlantic seaboard. Women were there as passive and inconsequential helpmates. Indians were wild and primitive peoples beyond the pale: unchanging objects of colonist's fears and aggressions. African slaves appeared as unfortunate aberrations in a fundamentally upbeat story of Englishmen becoming freer and more prosperous by colonizing open land. The other colonies of rival empires—Dutch, French, Spanish—were a hazy backdrop of hostility: backward threats to the English America that alone spawned the American Revolution and the United States......"

This is so accurate a description of my high-school view of history that I cringe in recognition. Thank goodness for the Civil Rights movement and the work of subsequent postmodern historians. Reading the newer volumes of American History has felt like a journey towards transparency and truth, at least in part. As more voices are heard about the reality of slavery and how it was resisted at every level by every enslaved person, white folk are better able to form a more accurate and comprehensive view of how our powerfully-white-country-of-English-speaking-men decide what we know and how we view the world we live in. It gives us the lens to be able to recognize and fight against the new version of slavery as seen in mass incarceration and race-based drug and voting-rights laws that affect people of color, or as Samuel Harrison was wont to say, people of a 'darker hue'. The narrow short-sighted-self-serving writing of history has done so much harm and it continues to perpetuate the same myths and same damage. To be ignored, discounted and shunned is stunningly painful; it is to deny the value of a human being, a race, or country of origin, or story. It is so much a part of what we continue to do that it seems almost impossible to break the cycle, dismantle the system that allows for this lopsided power.

In discovering the new view of American history that we are privy to today I realize that all history can never be known. But there are stories out there waiting to be told that will fill out our understanding of how the United States came to be. In school students primarily learn about the big events, wars, etc., not the details of an ordinary person's life, or local events that helped to shape a national event. So it is through biographies that each student has the opportunity to hear a story, a narrative and put it context with the larger events they learn in history class. It is through providing such information that students can hear the richer, more personal aspects that shape their world today. This book is such a biography.

After I moved to the Berkshire Hills of western Massachusetts and became interested in the history of place, I found so much untold information about the role of individuals in the building of America that I came to question what history is. All those dates (which I actually learn and remember easily) are just the scaffold upon which stories are hung. History is a collection of stories; a narrative about a time and a place, and the people and events that shape it. And the county I live in is a treasure trove of these untold stories that definitely shaped my own present.

The dictionary defines history as:
- 1, the branch of knowledge concerned with ascertaining and recording past events.
- 2, an oral or written narrative.

So then you have to ask: who tells the stories? And what stories are told? Who and what make it into the history books? Or, to use the words of the dictionary "who ascertains?" and "what is ascertained?" The obvious answer is: the people in power ascertain. And the story is the one they want told.

Really, though, history is fluid, changeable and re-writeable. It often takes hundreds of years for a complete picture to come out.

So, it is up to us, the people on the ground to get the rest of the stories out. And that is what is happening now. We will no longer tolerate being told what to think and how to view things. We will ascertain the stories/narratives and make them known far and wide. We can go back and discover the stories that were left untold. The archives and resources are thankfully still available.

This book is my attempt to participate in the re-writing of American history by telling the stories of African-American historic figures of Berkshire County, Massachusetts, so that these voices and stories also become a part of the backdrop of history.

I am deeply grateful to my son, Jonathan Barnes for his up-to-date perception and understanding of race relations today. His views and insights helped to shape this narrative. The writing of this book has been a personal journey of profound discovery from which I can never go back, nor would I want to. Social and racial justice has always been a theme in my life but now it is an all-consuming concern.

# HISTORICAL CONTEXT

Although we are taught that the founding of this country was based on religious freedom, nonetheless, each town that received permission to incorporate had to have enough funds to support a minister (Christian) and his family and build a church or meeting house. Religion was a large part of the life of every village and town. There was no media so people got together for worship at least every Sunday, if not on other days for revivals and prayer meetings, as well. They gathered together to sing, to dance, to socialize, to work, to pray, to eat. The life of each town was closely connected to the rhythms of the seasons as well as Christian religious holidays. Samuel Harrison's religious experiences must be taken in the context of his times.

The function of religious services and the role of music, especially song, in the 1800's is difficult for us to imagine today. At that time music was a way for people to connect and to communicate. Through song they were able to give expression to their feelings and sing of their joys and sorrows. Civil War songs played a large role in communication as well as reinforcing loyalty to the cause. And the church was a place where people gathered to be in community and share news. The ministers played a hugely important role in administering to the individuals in their congregations. The minister was often the only person to know how a family was getting along and what they might need, especially those left behind by a husband, son or father during the war. Today ministers play a similar role except to a much smaller segment of the population.

I have written this book based closely on Rev. Harrison's autobiography, *REV. SAMUEL HARRISON—His Life Story—As Told by Himself* and other of his written works. But I have, of course, taken great liberties in imagining conversations he might have had. Much of what I have imagined him saying is based on the articles and treatises he wrote while living in Pittsfield, MA.

And, looking at his photograph I inferred that he had a melancholy streak. And his birthday in April (Aries) led me to suppose that he had fire and energy with which to balance that tendency towards melancholy. His wife, Ellen, does not get mentioned much in his autobiography, but I know she played a decisive as well as supportive role in his life. She became more fully developed in my mind as the story unfolded. It was as if she were speaking through me. His 13 children, of whom only five survived to adulthood and only two survived him, are given shape in broad brush strokes that emerged from the situations members of the family found themselves in and that were described briefly in his autobiography. Two descendants of his, Ruth Edmonds Hill and Blayne Whitfield have both read and approved the manuscript so I don't think I have stretched the verity of the story too much.

The soldier, Isaiah Welch, whose voice and words I use in the conversations the soldiers have with Rev. Harrison, was actually mustered in the 55th Regiment. But his thoughts have been immortalized in a Philadelphia newspaper, the Christian Recorder, because he often wrote letters to the editor. He was a sergeant in his regiment. Much of what he and others 'say' in this book are from a letter to the editor on October 24th, 1863. Other letters to editors of other newspapers were also used as a basis for the conversations of the soldiers. Many of the letters were from "a member" of the 54th or 55th Regiment signed only with where they were from: Bay State (Massachusetts) or Pennsylvania or New York, i.e.:

"........Our debasement is most complete. No chances for promotion, no money for our families........., what is our incentive for duty? Yet God put it in our hearts to believe that we will survive or perish with the liberty of our country. If she lives, we live; if she dies we will sleep with her, even as our brave comrades now sleep with Col. Shaw within the walls of Wagner. More anon, Bay State."

(from [New York] Weekly Anglo-African, 30 April 1864)

The descriptions of the assault on Fort Wagner are mainly taken from Luis F. Emilio's record of the 54th Regiment: A BRAVE BLACK REGIMENT, The History of the 54th Massachusetts, 1863-1865. He commanded Company E and his record of the 3 years he was in charge was published in Boston in 1894.

The speech by Frederick Douglass is cobbled together from Douglass's own writings in the North Star. He was proudly invested in the 54th and 55th Regiments. Two of his sons, Lewis and Charles were mustered in the Regiments. Frederick Douglass wrote to the men of the 54th as they were training in Readville, Massachusetts before being sent to South Carolina:

"We can get at the throat of treason and slavery through the State of Massachusetts. She was first in the War of Independence; first to break the chains of her slaves; first to make the black man equal before the law; first to admit colored children to her common schools. She was the first to answer with her blood the alarm-cry of the nation when its capital was menaced by the Rebels. You know her patriotic Governor, and you know Charles Sumner. I need add no more. Massachusetts now welcomes you as her soldiers."........

I am so grateful for Luis Emilio's entire history of the 54th. The incredible detail provides a clear picture of the complexity behind the formation of "Colored Troops." There were so many specifics and firmly held attitudes about how they were to be formed that the fact of them is practically a miracle. Each step of the history of the 54th is recorded in detail.

And the book: Swamp Angels, a Biographical Study of the 54th Massachusetts Regiment, True Facts about the Black Defenders of the Civil War by Robert Ewell Greene was also a source of information.

"After the assault on Fort Wagner, Morris Island, South Carolina, July 18, 1863, Harriet Tubman, an underground railroad operator, a nurse and a Union spy went to Fort Wagner and assisted in the burial of the black soldiers and the white officers and cared for the wounded of the Fifty-Fourth Massachusetts Regiment." (Robert Ewell Greene)

It was primarily Massachusetts Governor John A. Andrew who was successful in petitioning for the formation of Black troops to fight in the War. But also the Secretary of War under Lincoln, Edwin M. Stanton and the Attorney General Edward Bates both firmly believed that African Americans, both free and enslaved (newly freed), should be given a soldier's status to fight in the war. Their support of Black Union troops helped persuade President Lincoln to sanction their formation. Their belief was also instrumental in making sure the soldiers received equal pay.

Eight of the photographs in the book are courtesy of the Massachusetts Historical Society. The photographs of the soldiers were collected by Capt. Luis F. Emilio, commander of Company E of the 54th Regiment and author of *A Brave Black Regiment, The History of the 54th Massachusetts, 1863-1865.* They date from circa 1860 to 1880 and include tintypes, one ambrotype, and albumen photographs depicting African-American members of the regiment. Permission to print granted by the Massachusetts Historical Society, in Boston, MA.

The photos of an older Samuel Harrison are courtesy of the Pittsfield Athenaeum in, Pittsfield, MA.

The one of a young Sam, as well as Ellen and Sam from their family bible, are courtesy of The Samuel Harrison Society on Third Street in Pittsfield, MA. The photographs of the Harrison Society were taken by me.

The photograph of the bronze Memorial to the 54th by Augustus Saint-Gaudens which is on Beacon Street in Boston, MA, opposite the State House is courtesy of National Park Service, Boston African American NHS.

The photograph of the "Soldiers of the 54th" was found on the *New England Historical Society* website where no credit is given. I both emailed and searched other sites for its origin but could find none. The same goes for the photograph of Sgt. William Carney and the lithograph of the assault on Fort Wagner on Morris Island by Kurz and Allison, 1890. If this is found to be not the case please contact me and I will make good.

## Chapter 1

The spring of 1861 was long in coming. All through March the city of Pittsfield remained in the grip of winter. The winds whipped through the thoroughfares and made the early spring flowers bend and twist with every gust. People hurried along North Street on their errands, barely able to keep their hats on. When Easter came on March 31st, the people of Berkshire County were uncertain how to celebrate this high holy day when talk of war was on everyone's lips. Do we pray for peace so that there is no fighting, bloodshed or deaths? Or do we pray for a war that could signal the end of slavery? Reverend Harrison decided to be as neutral as he could in his sermon and proclaim it was a time to let God's will be done. Good Friday was quiet and serious. Holy Saturday, the end of the somber season of Lent, was observed with quiet decorum. The sunrise service for Easter was also subdued. Everyone was waiting to hear what would happen. Would there be war? Would the president be able to reach a compromise? Would there be freedom for the people enslaved in the South without having to fight a war? No one knew and no one looked forward to finding out what a war would mean for the country.

~

Watching snow whip past his window the Reverend Samuel Harrison thought back on what had brought him to this place in his life, a minister in the all-Black Second Congregational Church in Pittsfield, Berkshire County, Massachusetts in 1861. What choices had he made, or rather, what choices had made him?

On the brink of war, a war that promised to break the back of the institution of slavery in the South finally and completely, he was a free man living in the North.

He had been born to enslaved parents forty-three years earlier. His parents, Jennie and William Harrison, had been born slaves in Savannah, Georgia. Their master's name was John Bolton. The Boltons owned a small plantation and Jennie Harrison worked as Mrs. Bolton's personal maid and William Harrison was the family coachman. The Bolton family had frequently visited Philadelphia where they owned a business. Sam had been born on one of those trips to Philadelphia on April 15th, 1818. Sometime after his birth the Bolton family returned to Savannah and decided to dismantle their plantation, release the people they had held in bondage and move north. Living in Georgia as they did, it was a complicated process to manage this. But for them it had become an economic necessity. Each enslaved person was given the option to remain in this country as a free person or to emigrate to Africa. Jennie and William chose to stay on in America. Just as Sam's parents received their emancipation papers Sam's father had died suddenly. It was a staggering turn of events for Jennie and Sam. With little recourse Jennie had asked to stay on as Mrs. Bolton's personal maid and move with the household and Sam to Philadelphia. A year later when the family moved to New York City, Jennie and Sam had moved there, as well, and lived in a tiny apartment on Liberty Street. To make ends meet Jennie took in piecework as a seamstress while continuing to work as Mrs. Bolton's maid, and Sam attended school.

Sam had no memories of what it was like to be enslaved. His mother chose to speak as little about those years as she could.

He had been curious about his father, though, and asked once what had happened to him.

"He was freed along with the rest of us, but then he went into the arms of the Lord," his mother had said. She had closed her eyes briefly. Sam knew this was a hard subject but he pressed on.

"Why did he die, Mama?"

His mother was silent for a few moments and then said, "Sam, soon after our emancipation your father got sick and the Boltons refused to pay for a doctor, saying we were on our own now. We didn't have any money at the time. That's why we couldn't get any medicine."

Sam digested this. Then he asked her, "Why did you stay with the Boltons then?"

"Well," his mother had shifted uncomfortably on her feet. "Well, I had no place to go. You and I were alone then. So I asked if I could continue to care for Mrs. Bolton. They said if I paid our way, or paid them back once we got to Philadelphia, then I could stay on to help the family ..."

His mother let out her breath in a deep sigh. They had been hard times, those first years in the north. Things were not a lot different in attitude towards Black people. But at least they were free and independent. She looked at Sam. "You understand now, son? Any more questions, Sam?"

Sam remembered that he had eventually been sent from New York City back to Philadelphia to live with his uncle who was a minister and shoemaker. His mother had married again. This man, Sam's step-father, proved to be an abusive alcoholic so Jennie had sent Sam, age nine, away for safekeeping. Once in Philadelphia Sam had immediately started learning the shoemaking trade. It had been a lonely life for a little boy. Two years later his mother had moved back to Philadelphia to be with him. She was a good seamstress and was able to make a living for the two of them. Sam had continued learning the shoe trade in his uncle's shop.

Sam's thoughts drifted to 1835 when he was seventeen.

He'd been working at his uncle's shoe shop for almost eight years and knew how to make a shoe from start to finish. He was proud of his accomplishments and knew he owed much to his mother.

She would receive the first pair of shoes he made completely on his own.

Getting ready to leave for the day Sam said, "Mama, you will have to come by the shop today. I have to choose the correct shoe-last for your feet! You can't put it off any longer!"

"Sam, I'll be there, I promise you! I'll be there near midday."

Sam nodded, excited to be in charge of his first pair of shoes from start to finish. He had already chosen the material, a soft glove-like leather the color of a ripe plum. He imagined the finished shoe, his mother slipping her foot into its elegant shape, fastening the silver buckle (or would she choose a velvet ribbon?), slipping the other shoe on and standing up, taking her first step in her new, brand new, custom-made shoes. He was proud that he had learned so much in the past five years. Here he was, seventeen years old and ready to step out on his own.

He hurried towards his uncle's shoe shop, his mind on the task ahead. As he approached Catherine Street he smelled something burning, something unpleasant. He was used to feeling uneasy walking through the Kensington neighborhood where so many people lived packed too close together. But today he saw two storefronts smashed in, windows broken and a banner ripped to smithereens. He knew one of the stores belonged to Mr. O'Malley who was a weaver from Ireland. He was nowhere in sight. There was a crowd of men standing in the street. Sam tried to pass by.

"Whatchu lookin' at, boy?" one of the men stepped menacingly towards Sam.

Sam, his eyes cast down, hastily picked his way around the broken glass, the pile of smoldering cloth that was mounded on the street. He didn't stop to inspect what had happened. But he could tell this had been an intentional act of destruction. He hurried on his way wondering what Mr. O'Malley had done to deserve that much hatred? Had the men in the street had anything to do with this? He had heard stories before of violent mobs attacking Black people and other people considered foreign, but had never before seen the results so clearly for himself. The working conditions in Philadelphia were never easy for newcomers. He knew the Irish were considered unwelcome immigrants. But this was a big country. There should be room for everyone. His heart was heavy and full of solemn feelings when he entered his uncle's shop. He tried to put these thoughts out of his mind for the time being. He needed to focus on the task at hand.

As he was sewing the soles onto a pair of shoes, he asked his uncle if he knew what had caused the disturbance the night before. Sam knew his uncle was a peaceful man with a strong sense of justice who often went out of his way to help those less fortunate than himself. And this included immigrants of any nationality newly arrived in Philadelphia. But everywhere was crowded. People did not have enough work. They were stuffed into tenements, often two or three families in one room. It was hard enough feeding their own families without new immigrants coming and taking up more space and competing for jobs. And all too often those jobs were underpaid.

"Well, Sam, Mr. O'Malley has the unfortunate luck to be from Ireland. It doesn't matter that he is a skilled weaver. His only crime is being Irish. The Irish are too new here to be liked and the people who came here first often feel frustrated and take it out on the newest arrivals."

"But Mr. O'Malley has been here a long time already," cried Sam.

"Yes, but he is Irish and he had something of value to destroy. Anger makes you do strange things, Sam. He could have employed some of the men; instead he has to start from scratch."

"Why don't the policemen help? Why didn't they protect Mr. O'Malley's shop?"

"Philadelphia doesn't know what to do about the new immigrants. We don't have a big enough police force to protect us all. And sometimes you get the feeling that they leave certain mobs alone to work it out for themselves. And firemen from one district do not put out fires in another. It is an unjust system. No one really benefits." His uncle sat down heavily at his workspace and began cutting out another pair of shoes. He sighed. "Nobody has it easy except a few rich folk," he muttered to himself.

Sam thought about injustice while he sewed. He knew that people of African descent met with a lot of the rage from the citizens of Philadelphia, whether they were doing anything or not. "Geography or the color of your skin," he thought, "and you were damned if you weren't white or if you came from the wrong place." He felt paralyzed with his inability to make matters right. He remembered being often taunted for the color of his skin. It felt all wrong. He resolved to try and help Mr. O'Malley that evening. Maybe if all the workers bonded together as one, something would change. As he continued sewing he realized that working with his hands, making something of use and beauty, helped to distract his mind. He was grateful to have a job like this.

§§§

Reverend Harrison had been in the Berkshire Hills of Massachusetts for eleven years. He reflected that although at first glance it did not seem that way, his journey towards the altar had been just about a straight line. The Second Congregational Church in Pittsfield was his first posting. He had been sent there at the behest of a committee of eight members of this newly formed Black church in January of 1850. He was comfortable in Pittsfield. The people were fond of him. And yet, on this Easter Monday in 1861, he felt a restlessness deep in his soul.

He knew the North was getting ready for a war, had manned fortifications in southern states and made ready to "defend the Union." He wanted to contribute practically to making slavery a thing of the past. He knew people of African descent needed to play a part in changing the course of history. But he knew not how he would be able to participate. How could he play a part, aside from speaking out for a "war of abolition" from his pulpit?

He thought back to the first time he had even considered the ministry as a vocation.

It was back in 1835 and his city of '*Un*-Brotherly Love,' Philadelphia, was in the midst of an immigration crisis. Irish families, escaping the famine in their homeland, were flooding the city looking for housing and work. Not only were they competing for jobs, but they were also Catholic in a mainly Protestant city. The tensions were often handled violently with little protection from the police force. The fears and anxieties of a crowded neighborhood were erupting in more property destruction and violence every night.

One evening, a few days after he had finished his mother's new shoes, Sam was preparing to go out. His neighborhood was in chaos. He wanted to help in some way. His mother protested, fearing for his safety.

"Sam, you must learn to choose your battles. Know what is important to you. You know in your heart that responding to every situation with such fire will only burn you out quicker."

Sam looked up at his mother; he was an egalitarian and hated injustice of any sort. "But mother, the workers are being beaten with brickbats! Mr. O'Malley's store is ruined. The firemen are not protecting them, they are out to hurt them! The Irish weavers have done no wrong. They only want a fair wage! And Uncle feels the same way. It's just wrong to treat a human being like that."

"This is not your battle, son. You are so young, still! You will have your own battles, ones that not only affect you, but also your people. There is injustice everywhere. Stay away from St. Mary Street tonight. I see no good coming of that action."

Sam looked at his mother with blazing eyes, "Mother! I know them! They work on our street! The police don't help! I think James will be there."

"Sam, Sam! You must stay away tonight. Stay home. Nothing good will come of this. I know it is hard but you mustn't get involved."

Sam knew when his mother was right. And knew he should listen to her. Suddenly he felt relieved. He would stay in, except to tell James he would not be going out.

"Can I trust you, Sam?

"Yes, Mama! You can."

Sam was still frustrated. His feeling for fairness, his dislike of violence, his loyalty to his people were strong forces in his soul. At seventeen why, oh why, wasn't he considered old enough to try and take matters into his own hands and join the fray? Churches had been burned, looters had invaded homes of innocent people. Philadelphians felt helpless and disenfranchised in their own neighborhoods. The fire departments selected which fires to put out and just let the others burn. It was unjust, and with no organized police force, it was chaos out there. He and James often discussed the situation late into the night. It wasn't right that people should be made to suffer so.

But his mother had been firm. Tonight he had some studying to do. And he had promised he would attend church with his mother the following morning. He sighed and took up his quill. Tonight he would stay at home. But he couldn't promise that he always would. He looked out the window at the evening sky as he sat at his desk, his books spread around him. The light from the moon cast a shadow that moved with the breeze on the curtains. He gazed outside, sighed, and bent over his books.

A week later Mrs. Harrison was encouraging Sam to attend an evening meeting at their church, the Second Presbyterian Church on St. Mary Street, a church composed of "colored persons."

"Sam, you would benefit with more churching! You know yourself that you get too caught up with what is going on in the outside world. This will bring you closer to God."

"The meetings are not to my taste, Mama, and you know that."

"Just this once. Just try again. They have that new speaker tonight, Reverend Porter. He comes from over Trenton in New Jersey; he speaks noble and inspiring words. You'd like him."

Sam knew his mother would not let this one go. It'd been the same old refrain for so long now, he could no longer honestly resist her urgings.

"Okay, Mama, just this once I'll go."

But when evening came Sam was out with James and their companions and remembered his promise too late. He just couldn't break away, no matter how bad he knew his mother would feel.

The next morning when his mother asked how it had gone he admitted he hadn't made it. She spoke sharply to him and he felt ashamed. She asked very little of him. Why couldn't he just go? He promised her he would go the next Monday evening.

And he did.

Now something strange and powerful occurred in that meeting, something Sam could never have anticipated. As the preacher spoke about the words of Christ: "Love one another" he felt an unseen power enter into his heart. A power that was both gentle and commanding. He was dazed. What was happening to him? He had never felt this way before. This was a different kind of preaching than what he was used to in childhood from Reverend Gillet. There was no fire and brimstone and the threat of hell and damnation if he misbehaved. This brought a sense of well-being, a sense of meaning and order to his heart and mind. He was curious. What was going on here? When he got home his mother asked him how it had been.

"I don't know, Mama, I can't really tell. I think it was okay. I can't really talk about it yet."

Then, to his mother's astonishment Sam decided to attend the next night's meeting. Again his heart was touched as though by an angel wing.

"The Lord welcomes you to open your heart to his love ... He will be with you always until the end of time ... All your prayers will be heard ... Ask and it will be given to you, seek and you will find, knock and the door will open." It felt gentle and welcoming.

When Reverend Porter invited anyone in the congregation to come before the altar and kneel down and accept the Savior into their hearts, Sam, to his own surprise, joined them. Kneeling before the altar he felt something for the first time in his life: a deep, abiding peace entered his heart. Suddenly he knew what he wanted to be. He knelt for a long time, deeply musing. When he came home his mother was waiting.

"And, how was it!"

"I'm a new person," Sam replied solemnly.

His mother looked at him skeptically. "What do you mean?"

"I'm a new person. I am someone who knows what he wants to do!"

"Yes, and what's that?" she asked, looking at him with a little more trust.

"I've found God and His only begotten son, the Christ ... I'm changed ... I think I'd like to become a minister!"

His mother, stunned, cried out in joy! "Oh Sam, oh Sam, this is wonderful! This is my heart's desire! I've prayed for this very thing. You've filled my heart with joy." Tears were rolling down her cheeks as she folded Sam into her arms and then suddenly pulled back, looking up at his face. "You're not messing with me, are you?"

When Sam shook his head she said: "Sam! You couldn't make me happier! Can you tell me a little about what happened?"

"Ask and you shall receive! Your prayers, Mama, have been answered! And I myself could not be more surprised!"

"But what went on in your heart, Sam?"

"Well," he said, "it is hard to describe. As I was kneeling there, something changed in me. My heart opened and I felt love streaming towards me. No, not streaming, it was more like filling me up from the inside. It was as if I knew for the first time who I was." He paused and, looking at his mother, continued. "You know how they say you are "converted"? Well I didn't feel converted. I felt I could finally see who I truly am. I felt recognized ... and *seen*, as well. I could feel my true self. It's a strange thing, Mama to go through life half asleep and then suddenly you wake up and everything is different, you're different. The world is the same but you are different ..." He trailed off. His mother took his hands in hers and kissed both his palms. "I don't know what to say ... I am so pleased. I'm astounded."

Sam went to bed as if in a dream. He went through the motions of getting ready for sleep as if guided by an unseen hand. He fell asleep the minute his head hit the pillow.

### §§§

"Praises sing to God!" Sam hummed as he got ready for the day. He felt giddy with joy. He would stop by James' before work. He wanted to speak about his experience to someone, to see if it was real, if someone else could understand what he was saying. He and James had been friends since childhood and James was a good listener. Trying his new experience on him seemed a sensible first step.

"I never thought of myself as a religious person, you know that! And I can't really say this is a religious feeling. It's so real to me and religion always felt like something outside of me. This is inside me. This is who I am ..."

James nodded and said sagely: "I always knew you had a side to you that was drawn to higher things, Sam! This isn't strange to me, hearing about your experience! It makes me feel like I'd like to come with you next Monday and see what happens to me! You know my mother'd welcome that, as well!"

"James! What an idea! It'd be great if you came."

They parted, promising to meet in front of the church on Monday.

As they entered the church and made their way towards

the pews they saw Reverend Porter standing in the aisle. His manner was so welcoming, warm and reverential that it put Sam in high spirits. He introduced James and they sat down towards the front. He and James nodded at Ellen, a young girl Sam and James had known since childhood. She looked over at them from the other side of the aisle, waved, and then lowered her eyes self-consciously. Sam smiled and waved and then turned his attention to Reverend Porter as he stepped up to the pulpit. Silence descended on the church.

Again Reverend Porter emphasized a loving God who gave his only begotten Son to remind humankind where they came from, to remember their heavenly home. His focus this time was on the Sermon on the Mount where Christ gave his disciples the Lord's Prayer. Sam kept glancing at James to see if he could gauge his reaction to the service. James' eyes were closed and he was sitting very still. Sam couldn't tell what was going on inside him. He knew it might take a while for James to know his path. He wondered if James would see the difference between this loving God and the one they knew from their childhood pastor, Reverend Gillet's sermons. Reverend Gillet was always goading them to resist the Devil, keep on the straight and narrow path or they would be punished in some way. His God seemed a distant judge rather than a savior or friend.

Reverend Porter repeated "God is love. Whoever abides in Love abides in God and God in him." What a different message. This minister was coming at it from another side. He was telling them that in order to be good, God gave all humanity his everlasting love and the strength to carry on. He never gave people trials beyond the capacity of their strength. Sam glowed with a newfound sense of power. Again everyone was invited to come forward to receive the Savior into their hearts. Both James and Ellen remained seated while others went forward. "It's not their time, yet," Sam thought to himself.

After the meeting Reverend Porter invited Sam to officially become a member of the church. At first Sam was put on probation to prove his sincerity and then, during communion three months later, he was admitted to the church. He was eighteen years old.

# Chapter 2

Sam had a plan. He hadn't had much schooling but if he wanted to become a minister he would have to have at least three more years of education. Through a recommendation from Reverend Porter, the American Education Society heard of Sam's hard work and wishes for furthering his education. They offered to pay his way to the Gerrit Smith School in Peterboro, New York.

Gerrit Smith was a philanthropist, an abolitionist and a supporter of human rights. As an abolitionist he considered the enslavement of human beings to be the vilest of all human customs. He reviled what was called "chattel slavery." In the United States in the 1830s there were over a million enslaved people owned by White people, mainly in the South. Gerrit Smith, who was white, believed in education as a way out and up from slavery. He set up his school on the system of manual labor. That meant that the students, who were all of African descent, went to school for part of the day, usually in the mornings and also worked for part of the day helping on the estate but also learning a trade. They received their meals and a bed and an education in exchange for their work.

He declared that his students were "encouraged in freedom of thought and actions ..." He was an idealist who wanted to "turn back the tide of prejudice."

§§§

Sam looked around his room, searching for what he could wear when he was away at school. Suddenly his clothes looked shabby to him. How could he go out among the people, take a trip by train in the worn clothing he saw hanging on the rod. He would need a new suit.

"Mama," he said, "I have decided to work with Uncle on the shoe bench a while longer. I need to be able to buy some decent cloth for you to make me a new suit. For work I can wear my day clothing but for class I must look a decent man."

His mother, who knew Sam had also been earning some money selling subscriptions for a Dr. Brisbane who owned a new abolitionist newspaper in Philadelphia, began laying out a pattern for a new suit. Sam had grown so in the past few years that she had to start the suit from scratch. Within a few days she had found just the right fabric and started on the cutting and sewing. Sam brought her his weekly earnings and soon there was enough to pay her back for the cloth. She realized his ambition to become a minister had taken on a life of its own. She was very proud.

"Sam, try this on," his mother said. "I need to check the length of the sleeves and the legs."

Soon the suit was finished. Sam went about organizing his trip to Peterboro. He would take the train north and then hire a carriage to take him the last leg of the trip.

Finally he was ready and the day of leave-taking from his mother had dawned. Suddenly he wasn't so sure that he wanted to leave his home. Putting on a brave face he came into the hallway to get his coat. His mother was standing by the door, a handkerchief in her hand. She had been weeping, he could see.

"Mama, this is hard! I don't know if I should go. What will become of you?"

"Sam," she said, "I'm so proud of you. This is the way of things. You are now a man and you'll make your mark on the world if you keep your mind on your books and follow a straight path. Don't worry about me. I've got my work, my friends, your uncle and of course my God and my church."

"I know you do, Mama, but what about every evening? Who'll you talk to?"

"It's alright. I feel at ease in my heart now, even though I'll be missing you sorely. I'll get accustomed to being alone. No worries, it'll be alright. And you'll write to me. And I'll write to you."

He put his arms around her and they stood there for a long time. Then he stepped back, took his suitcase in his hand and opened the door.

"Godspeed, my son. You're so dear and so good. I know you'll do well."

Sam was touched by his mother's words and deepened his resolve to take the opportunity to have an education very seriously.

"Good bye, Mama! I'll miss you too! And I will make you proud."

Next he said goodbye to James. James was working as a blacksmith and was very happy in his choice of profession. Horses were such noble creatures and he had a way with them. "Hey Sam! I'll miss you. I know you'll be a good preacher one day, I just know it. I'll keep your seat warm at the church."

Sam punched him on the shoulder, then shook his hand and made his way down the street towards the train station.

When he arrived in Peterboro he was introduced to his teachers, given his books, shown his room and met the other students. Finally to be among other young people who were also devoted to their books, and intent on getting a good education. Many of them were farm boys, strong of arm and used to working hard. Sam had worked hard all his life, but not like this! This was a challenge.

In the afternoons, after classes, they were set digging ditches to drain a swampy part of Mr. Smith's land. Sam's hands were blistered and his arms ached every evening. Maybe he wasn't as strong as some of the other boys, but he knew he could keep up.

The schooling was just what he had dreamed of: classes in history and literature, philosophy, practical math and even English grammar. He and the other students often stayed up long into the night discussing their classes, arguing philosophical fine points about the meaning of life and their dreams for the future. They had all experienced the pain of oppression, prejudice and injustice in various ways. This was a safe haven to speak about other things, things that brought them meaning and strength.

"I'm reading an American scholar who writes very inspiringly!" said Sam to the group. "Even though he is white, he speaks moral truths that don't differentiate between white and brown skin!"

"And who is this scholar? Do I know him?" asked an older student.

"Well, Mr. Smith gave me a special assignment to write an essay on Ralph Waldo Emerson," replied Sam.

"Oh! Yes! I've read him! He's what they call a transcendentalist, someone who doesn't bow to the outdated traditions of the Old World," said Elymus Rogers, also an older student. "I like reading him. He urges us to become independent thinkers, to break the old molds and be bold and step out of our outworn past."

"That would mean to me that there should no longer be any persons who are not free. It's old and outworn to think that one man can own another man and tell him what to do ... and whip him when he doesn't," responded Sam thoughtfully.

There was silence in the room as the students thought about such a time when all people, created equal as they were, would be free.

"What do you think, Sam? Does Mr. Emerson give you any ideas how to make a better world?" asked the first student.

"We need to pioneer a new way of looking at our fellow human beings. How do we do that, you ask? Become teachers and writers, and moralists. Don't be afraid to speak out!"

Being young and idealistic, this sounded like good advice.

"It could work," said another student, "writing books and treatises like Mr. Emerson. It would also be a way to reach people and teach them a more uplifting way of thinking."

"Well, I guess learning English grammar will help with that," exclaimed Sam, who did not like parsing sentences. "It'll help when I want to write sermons, I guess, although I don't think many people care that much."

"Yeah, the learned types care, but the rest of the folk? I don't know. And they're the ones we wanna reach. The ones who need their minds elevated." said Elymus.

"Well, the ones we wanna reach are the ruffians and they don't read. It's a real dilemma. I guess we have to become good speakers or preachers, really good talkers," said the older student.

Still having homework to do, the young men went back to their studies.

The mind and the body were each given a good workout and the students thrived under all the attention given to their development.

Every evening they joined the faculty in the dining hall where the food was plentiful and good. There were luscious apple orchards, many different fruit trees and a large vegetable garden. Mr. Smith's stately home sat atop a green meadow that sloped down to a stream running through the property. There were also terraces of grapes in a productive vineyard. Mr. Smith wanted to cultivate the entire twenty-five acres of land. Draining the swamp would create more land to be farmed. The work was hard but the rewards were equal in measure.

His new friend Elymus Rogers also wanted to become a minister. They often sat side by side at the dining table and discussed their plans for the future.

"Have you ever heard of Reverend Porter of Trenton, New Jersey, by any chance?" asked Sam one evening when he and Elymus were discussing the ministry. "He's the person who changed the course of my life."

"I don't know him, but I've heard his name. What about him do you like so much?"

"Well, he has a way about him that brings peace to my heart. He was able to explain passages in the Bible in a way that made my life and my experiences more comprehensible," replied Sam.

Elymus had a few years of solid education already behind

him and he was committed to a particular ministry in New Jersey where they were awaiting his return so that he could start his training. His knowledge of the Bible was far greater than Sam's.

"That's very useful," he said, "especially since we of African descent are subjected to so many indignities. That God meant us to be a race of servants to the white man is nowhere written in the Bible. I intend to use the word of God as a sword to strike down prejudice and injustice until it is gone!" he said hotly.

§§§

"Men! Men! Quiet down! I have an announcement to make," called out Gerrit Smith.

They were in the dining hall having the evening meal. The students were talking among themselves as they dipped bread into their potato and leek soup.

"On Thursday evening next we will have special guests come to address the school. I want everyone to attend. These two guests are the most famous women in America!"

There was murmuring among the students. It was a rare event to hear outsiders speak, and women at that!

Elymus Rogers quipped, "And what would two *women* have to say to us?"

Mr. Smith smiled. "These are the Grimké sisters of Charleston, South Carolina. They have left their slave-owning family and come north to work for the abolition movement. They are causing quite a furor amongst not only slave owners, but also citizens of the North who do not think women should speak in public. I do believe they have been banned from their home city!"

"*What* is causing the furor in the North then?" asked Sam? "That *women* are speaking out? Or that they are against

22

slavery?"

"They not only speak against slavery for the Anti-Slavery Society but they are also crusaders for the rights of women. The right to vote, the right to own property, the right to go out in public without a chaperone, to have equal rights as men. They say they won't be silenced while waiting for slavery to be abolished," replied Mr. Smith. "They are brave women. Come and hear them speak!"

And so they all did. The men were curious to see and hear what women such as Angelina and Sarah Grimké would say. Women having the same rights as men was an alien topic!

The hall was full, with every seat taken. The students and faculty alike were talking loudly amongst themselves until Sarah and Angelina Grimké stepped onto the stage. There was a sudden and complete silence as the two women looked out over their audience of Black and White Americans.

"I stand before you as a southerner, exiled from the land of my birth by the sound of the lash and the piteous cry of the slave. I stand before you as a repentant slaveholder," proclaimed Angelina, the younger of the two sisters. "I was born on a plantation, in Charleston, South Carolina, the youngest of fourteen children. All fourteen of us, including our parents, were cared for by Black slaves, old, young, male, female. These people of African descent had to do our every bidding. They had no choice. Our parents owned them, each and every one. I know firsthand what this type of bondage does to the human spirit. I could do nothing to make our parents understand the immoral nature of this practice and so I came north to Philadelphia with my sister, Sarah." She cleared her throat and stood silently for a moment, seeming to be thinking about her next words. When she began speaking again her voice was more persuasive, less exclamatory.

"Now, we are Christian women, Quakers, and we know the teachings of Christ, and his message of love. Nowhere does He state that skin color determines ones' status in society. Nor does He state that women are inferior to men. But does our society reflect these premises? Were we women created as gifts to men for their possession or enjoyment? No! Nor were you," and she pointed towards the audience, where the Black students were sitting separately from the faculty, "created to serve the white man. Women are unique and intelligent beings, capable of independent thought, of caring for themselves. And you, originally of the continent of Africa! Are you not independent, autonomous human beings torn from a culture where you were lords and masters of your own kingdoms? Are we not, all of us, deserving of equal rights and responsibilities as white men?"

She paused again, smiling.

"Where does the Bible claim this is not the case? Women are bound to God alone. We are not bound to men, neither our husbands, our fathers, our sons or our brothers. But our society has made it so. And, our society proclaims chattel slavery to be destiny and women to be subservient to men. Women are viewed as the possessions of men to be admired for her personal charms and caressed and humored like a spoiled child or converted into a mere drudge to suit the convenience of her lord and master. Does that not give us a natural bond with female Black slaves?"

The audience drew a collective in-breath as Angelina made the comparison. This was high talk, indeed. Almost too much to digest. But these two sisters were courageous speakers, making statements no one could in all honesty refute. The audience hung on their every word.

§§§

That evening after the Grimké sisters had gone the students gathered in the dining hall to discuss the evening's talk.

"What do you think? Are women oppressed?" asked Elymus.

"Not any more than we are!" replied Sam.

"We are withheld the right to vote, but we can own property. And, we have access to education and employment." said Richard Miller, another friend of Sam's.

"Yes, but we are free up here in the North, at least some of us are. In the South not one enslaved person has any of those rights!" said Samuel Nelson.

"I know, I know. But is it a good move to harness equal rights for women to the cause of abolition? Won't the one slow the other down if a person does not agree with both?" asked Richard.

"Could be, but I say they're brave women to go about the country speaking in public," said Elymus. "I know my parents would be scandalized to hear that a woman is standing in front of a crowd of strangers, especially a mixed crowd of men and women. I myself found them mesmerizing!"

"My parents are also not so progressive as to think women should be expressing those kinds of ideas in public," said another student.

"Well, they are doing it and I, for one, am not going to stop them. I know Frederick Douglass is behind the idea of women's suffrage," said Sam. "I would think it is an individual decision to get behind one or the other. We need both causes if this country is to move forward."

The mood at the school was one of heightened interest in

the cause of abolition as well as women's rights. The Grimké sisters visit left a residue of hope that change was on the way. Each student buckled down to his studies, hoping to become a part of the change.

~

The men worked in the mornings bringing in the harvest. The grapes were handled professionally by people hired from the town but everyone could participate in the apple harvest and cider making. Squashes, pumpkins, beets, potatoes, onions, garlic, all were gathered in and stored in root cellars and barns. There was a feast of thanksgiving at the end of September with music, cider, donuts, apple pie, pumpkin pie and much gaiety and laughter. Their stomachs full of good food and their heads full of learning, discussion, talks on new subjects, the students were content.

Then, suddenly in late October, when the leaves on the maple trees lining the drive were in full color, the students found out that the school was closing. They could no longer remain and receive an education. No reason was given. Understandably the whole school was very distressed, including the teachers. Five of the students, including Sam and Elymus sent Gerrit Smith a letter saying: *"None of us has escaped the sword of prejudice or the scourge of oppression, and all of us have been compelled to walk in the valley of degradation. Hence all of us value this institution very highly, and we ask with one united voice that our school may continue one year longer."*

Gerrit Smith was in complete sympathy with his students but was not able to grant their wish. However, he made arrangements for those students who wanted to go on with their education to transfer to other schools. Mr. Smith recommended to Sam, and his two friends, Richard Miller and Samuel Nelson, that they attend a preparatory school in Ohio on the Western Reserve.

"But, how will we get there?" Sam questioned.

"If you are serious about going, I will arrange your passage to Ohio," Mr. Smith offered. "It will take a few days by wagon, canal boat, steamer and the last few miles will be on foot. But it is doable. I will help with the finances for the trip."

The young men were very grateful and assured Mr. Smith that they were indeed serious about this new opportunity.

"Well, then, consider it arranged. I apologize for the necessity of this trip. I would that the school could remain open. For now, though, it's just not possible. Good luck in your future endeavors, men. I wish you Godspeed."

Mr. Smith went to make the arrangements while Sam and his friends got ready to go.

It was windy and cold on the day they started out. They had no idea what was in store for them. Sam had written to his mother explaining their plan. He promised he would write when they arrived in Ohio. Sam was glad his friends were coming, too, as none of them had ever traveled this far alone. They packed their belongings and set out the next day. The first part of the trip was uneventful. Eight miles by wagon took them to the Erie Canal. After purchasing tickets, they boarded a line-boat that was pulled by mules and horses on a towpath that followed the entire canal. It went all the way to Buffalo. The cost was 1½ cents per mile at a distance of about 360 miles.

"Where can we get something to eat?" Sam asked another passenger. "Oh, you can buy crackers, cheese, cake or pie from vendors along the tow path, every few miles" was the reply. So they spent a few pennies and ate a hearty supper of meat pie, a wedge of cheese and a few apples. To drink they shared a bottle of cider. Then they went below to find their berth to sleep for the night. Having climbed into three neighboring berths, they were close to sleep when they heard the captain ask, quite audibly, as if in a sudden afterthought: "Does anyone object to having these colored men sleep in the cabin?" Sam's stomach clenched. But no one replied and so he relaxed and was able eventually to fall asleep. He had become so accustomed to the egalitarian atmosphere of the school that he had forgotten how much it hurt to hear someone single him out as different or not equal. There were no further overt incidents of prejudice on the boat.

In the evening of the second day they reached Buffalo where they disembarked. The plan was for them to take a steam ship to Cleveland, Ohio, next morning.

"We will have to find a place to spend the night," said Richard. "Who'll take us in?"

"Well, we do have the funds! I think cold coins will do the trick," countered Sam.

At the first boarding house Sam knocked confidently at the door.

"What you want?" asked the woman, eyeing the three of them. "We ain't got no room for the likes of you!" she said coldly and closed the door in their faces.

Hungry and cold after knocking on many another door, they finally found a lodging house that was sympathetic to their plight. They were shown to a cold room in the attic.

"I can see stars through the roof." Sam exclaimed, disappointed.

"And it's cold!" Richard rejoined, "but we'll live through

it!" They knew this was true and bundled up in the blankets that had been set out for them. The shame of being turned away from four other places stung and it was a long time before they fell asleep.

The next morning they boarded the steamship to cross Lake Erie. Being late October it was very cold. The wind blew incessantly. They were not given any place to get out of the wind and rain. There were two cabins, but the sailors said "No entry here for you! Go below deck where the steerage people are."

Sam and his friends went below deck to steerage, but it was so crowded and filled with German immigrants on their way west that they decided to stay on deck and hide themselves behind barrels. The going was so rough that the ship had to put in at several ports along the route.

Finally they were able to go ashore in Cleveland. They found a wagon and driver who agreed to carry them the 24 miles to Hudson, Ohio, and their school, Case Western Academy, for $7. They were so relieved to have finally reached their destination. At last they would be continuing the education they craved.

~

Upon arrival in Ohio Sam and his friends knew that, in order to pay for the school, as well as room and board, they would have to find work. Sam knew he could always ply his trade on the shoe bench. Richard found employment with a farmer and Sam Nelson worked with a house painter. Sam took a job in a shoe shop in the village. They each felt secure knowing they would have the money now to pay for their books and living expenses. All three would be earning six cents an hour. Professor Rufus Nutting invited them to dine with his family until they found accommodations, which they soon did in the Preparatory School dormitory where classes were also held.

And so began their schooling. They studied Greek and Latin, mathematics, elocution, philosophy, theology and history. They had classes with the White students, who initially showed frustration at being asked to share their studies with Black folk.

"Where'd they come from?" Sam heard one of them say. He looked around and noticed that they were the only Black people in the room. He sighed.

It appeared that the teacher had also heard the remark because suddenly he heard him say:

"These men have come from the Gerrit Smith School in upstate New York," said Professor Laurens Hickock. "They will be attending classes with you. See that you make them feel welcomed."

Some of the students looked sheepish, while the rest kept their eyes steadily forward and did not look at Sam or his two friends. After a few weeks, though, their intolerant behavior lessened. Only a few of the White students continued to show their displeasure at having to share their classes with "Negroes" and the atmosphere eventually became more relaxed.

To finally feel accepted on the merits of their personalities and not judged by their race made their experience at the school doubly meaningful. It also made it harder when Sam subsequently found out that the owner of the shoe shop where he worked, did not believe in 'Negro education.' He tried to make Sam work all the time so that he wouldn't have time to study. When Sam realized what was going on he quit and began working for his favorite teacher, Professor Hickock, who paid him to cut and split firewood as well as do odd jobs around the academy. This he did for the remaining three years he was at the school.

Finally he was ready to return home to Philadelphia. He had met his goals and become an educated man. His mind had been molded by fine, humanitarian-minded professors, as well as the many discussions and debates with his fellow classmates and in seminar. His opinions and views on life and liberty had grown to reflect his own deep sensibilities: his sense of integrity, justice and ethics. He felt ready to start his life back home in the East.

*Samuel Harrison*

# Chapter 3

It was 1839. Times had changed since Sam had left for New York State and Ohio. Immediately upon arrival he felt even greater tension and unrest in his home city of Philadelphia. His mother brought him up to date about the changes she had experienced while he was gone.

"I don't know what to think!" she told him. "It's a good thing that people are talking about the evils of slavery. Raising people's awareness is always good, but it's become too volatile a topic." She sighed. "It's dangerous to be an abolitionist now too, Sam. No one is safe anymore. I know that those of us colored folk who are free are often attacked for no reason. But white men, too, are attacked for being abolitionists. No one is safe here anymore."

Sam and his mother were sitting at the kitchen table eating his first meal back at home. He remembered the meat pie from his younger days. Meat and vegetables in a crumbly buttery crust.

He sighed and took a long drink of cider. His mother went on, "And we have a new wave of people from Europe. Not just Irish folk but people from Poland are coming over. It must be real bad in Poland for them to want to live here."

"Do you ever see anything of Mr. O'Malley?" Sam inquired.

"He's back, yes. But he seems more timid, almost fragile. He closes shop before dark and only hires Irish folk."

Sam knew conditions for the newest immigrants were even more crowded and unsanitary than in the years before he left, and that paid work was hard to come by. He was grateful to have his uncle's shoe shop to fall back on. He took heart. He was going to study for the ministry. His work would be tending to people's souls. He would be helping people, consoling the lost, the ill, the sick at heart. His work would hopefully aid in finding peaceful resolutions to conflict and suffering. He would be contributing to the cause of justice in a non-tangible way. Non-tangible but no less vital.

Despite the conditions he was glad to be back on familiar ground with people he knew. James was finished with his apprenticeship and had his own blacksmithing business in the Mount Airy district. He had not seen him yet.

"I'm still interested in becoming a minister, Mama, but first I have to make some money," he said.

"You'll find a way, dear, I'm sure. You always have the shoe trade."

"Yes, I know that. But why shouldn't I try and use my education and find work somewhere where my learning is valued?"

"What do you have in mind?"

"I'd like to work somewhere with books, with people who like to discuss literature, or even religion or philosophy!"

"I see," said his mother quietly. "That sounds different and very interesting."

This man, this son of hers, was so grown up, so confident

and purposeful that she didn't want to stand in his way. "It certainly seems better than being treated like a sub-human, like I am sometimes," she thought. "If I have to mend any more dresses for Mrs. Giles, I will spit!" Jennie reflected on the last time Mrs. Giles had brought back a dress she had mended only days before.

"What have you done to my dress, you, you, miscreant?" she had sputtered. "I spent good money to have this seam repaired and now, now look at it!"

Jennie had looked at it and tried to say it was a new rip.

"New rip? A new rip? You calling me a liar? I'll have you reported!"

Jennie had made a sound like the blowing out of a candle and had taken the dress from the woman wordlessly. She would mend it again. And not get paid. Her heart burned in her chest. It was a privilege to be ignorant of the evils of economic and racial distinctions. "It will be different for Sam," she thought. "Different because he will have more opportunities now to work with more elevated and educated people." Her heart felt less burdened. Her son's life would be different.

After many days and inquiries Sam heard there was an opening at a bookstore next to Market Street with a Mr. Judah Dobson.

"Mama, the clientele, the people who buy books there are some of the foremost ministers of the city. Reverend Porter is known to come there."

"Ah! Then it must be a central hub of learning, no?" she asked teasingly.

"I've been offered a room above the shop, my meals taken with the Dobson family. I know you'll miss me but I'll be working during the days and studying at night. I'll try to visit often. It's not so very far."

Jennie smiled. She knew it was time for her son to be completely on his own. It was the right order of things. "I'm fine with that, Sam. I'm just pleased to have you near once again!"

Sam moved his few possessions over to his new room above the bookstore. During the day he helped Mr. Dobson with whatever tasks needed doing. He often participated in the many lively discussions that arose with the customers and frequently spoke about his schooling in Ohio and his desire to further his studies to become a minister. Within a month he knew the book trade well enough to be left in charge of the store while Mr. Dobson went on trips to other booksellers and attended conferences on a variety of subjects. He was an abolitionist desiring to spread the word about the horrors of slavery.

"Theodore Weld's book *American Slavery As It Is* is causing quite a stir. It is sure to be reprinted soon with so many copies flying off the shelves!" he said to Sam the day before he was to leave on one of his frequent journeys.

"Uh hunh, I've seen it here, but not looked at it yet," said Sam.

"Well, it's interesting in the way it's drafted. It takes the wording of actual advertisements for runaway slaves written by Southern slave owners, as well as southern newspaper articles to chronicle one of the darkest sides of slavery, the break-up of families, the indifference the southern White man shows towards the bond between a mother and her child, a father and his children, his wife. It does a good job of highlighting

the callous dividing up of families to make a profit off of a slave family."

"I'll be sure to take a look at it this evening. Elymus, my friend from the Gerrit Smith School, Elymus Rogers, has written me about it and would like to come one day and discuss its contents with some of your customers," replied Sam. "Theodore Weld is the husband of one of the Grimké sisters, I believe, Angelina Grimké. They came and spoke at our school when we were there."

"Is that so? Well, you must read the book then. It'll be of great interest! Now I must be off."

~

One day on an errand for Mr. Dobson Sam saw Ellen Rhodes leaving a shop on Catherine Street. She was a friend from childhood who had been orphaned when quite young. He had lost track of her in the years since they both attended Rev. Porter's services at the Presbyterian Church. "Ellen!" he called over to her, "I haven't seen you in so long! How are you?"

Ellen looked up startled and her cheeks suffused with a warm glow. She stopped and waited for him to cross the street so they could talk. "Hello, Sam!" she said looking him up and down. "You look mighty grown up!" Sam, caught unawares by her confident greeting, smiled broadly. "And you look like a sight for sore eyes!" he parried with a smile. She looked at him measuringly.

"How long've you been back, Sam, I knew you'd been away for a while."

I've been back about two months," he replied. "And you? What are you doing with yourself these days?"

"I live at the girls boarding house on Montrose Street. I'm working as a seamstress. You?"

"I am working at a bookstore near Market Street. Mr. Judah Dobson owns it."

"Oh! That sounds delightful! To be among books all day! That suits you, doesn't it?"

Sam was glad she seemed to know what suited him.

"I'm on an errand and cannot bide for too long. Would you be able to go for a stroll down Market Street later this evening?" he suggested.

Ellen took a moment as if to reflect on her schedule. She looked at him through lowered eyelashes, "I would like that very much. How about 7:00 p.m. this evening. We can walk to the park."

With that settled Sam continued reluctantly on his way, looking back at Ellen as he made his way to the bookstore.

A few weeks later, on a visit to his mother, he regaled her with tales from the bookstore.

"Oh Mama, I'm so pleased with my new work. I'm not only among books but I also have time to study more. There are many books on theology that get me thinking and thinking. And clergy are always coming to buy books. Why just yesterday I entered into discussion with a Methodist minister and he was able to set me straight on a couple of difficult passages in the book I was reading."

Sam's mother smiled. She was pleased to have her son nearby again. And to have him happy in his work was almost too much to hope for. Now, if only he could find himself a wife!

"Sam," she said, "have you thought of settling down and starting a family?"

Sam looked at his mother quizzically. How did she always know what was in his heart? How was she able to read him so accurately?

"Well, Mother," Sam smiled, "funny you should ask. I've run into Ellen again. You remember her?"

His mother looked at her son. Will he never cease to surprise her? "Of course I remember Ellen! Ellen Rhodes. I remember she lived in the orphanage downstreet." She smiled. "And what do you think of her, if I may ask?"

"Well, we get on quite famously. We've walked out now quite a few times. She's shy, but I think she likes me."

"Oh Samuel Harrison! And when were you going to tell me?"

"Why, I'm telling you now!" he replied teasingly.

He and Ellen saw each other almost daily. They met at his mother's home in the evenings and went to church on Sundays. Very quickly they each knew that they had found the person with whom they would like to spend the rest of their lives.

"What're your dreams, Ellen? If you could have anything?" asked Sam one evening while sitting on the porch outside his mother's house.

"That's a curious question!" she replied looking up at his face. "If you want to know I have modest ambitions. I want a family; I want a home to bring them up in. I want a safe world for them to live in, a world that does not judge on the color of your skin. I want a husband who is happy in his work and who comes home in the evening wanting to be there with his family." She smiled at him. "Modest, right?"

"Not modest, neither foolish, dear Ellen! Humble wishes, wishes no one should have to wish for! They should be self-evident," said Sam. "I'll do what I can to play my part in your dreams Ellen! And perhaps, just perhaps the rest can happen too!"

"What are your dreams, dear Sam?" asked Ellen, settling her head against his shoulder the better to listen to what she assumed would be a long discourse. She knew Sam had high ideals and great imaginings for his future.

"Well, first as you know, I'd like to be an ordained minister with my own congregation." He paused, his eyes closed, the better to see into the future. "I too would like a large family. Being only one all my life gives me a hankering to hear the sounds of many children's voices! But I also think I'd like to be able to travel a bit, see more of our country. I liked Ohio, but I hanker after mountains, like the Alleghenies or maybe the Catskills. It was pleasant during the hot months when we were at Mr. Smith's school. Not hot like here." Sam was silent for a while. "But what about you, yourself Ellen? What would you like for yourself?"

She looked at him questioningly. "Why, Sam, I told you. Nothing would give me more pleasure than making a home for my family. That is enough for me, rest assured."

Sam remained in Judah Dobson's employ for eight months, continuing to learn the ins and outs of the book trade while also studying for the ministry. It was a daily opportunity to be among learned men concerned with national events as well as with matters concerning the soul and the presence of God in all human beings. When spring came he felt he needed to earn more money so that he and Ellen could afford to get married. He started working again for a shoemaker on South Third Street, earning enough to set up his own shop. He also began teaching Sabbath classes at a local church and became known for his speaking skills. He had seen and experienced enough of racism and oppression to feel entitled to preach about social justice and equality. He spoke quite eloquently to his Sabbath classes, his fervent voice ringing on in the hearts of the people who heard him.

"When I was young, or rather younger," he told his class, "I did not understand the value of going to church and our minister did nothing to make me think differently. He was always talking about sin. Then, there were violent outbreaks near the church my mother went to and I saw great and needless suffering. People's businesses burned down, people died and their homes were destroyed. The riots seemed to start for no apparent reason. No one particular event triggered it. But, then I realized it was a way for people who felt powerless over the condition of their lives to feel some sort of control. They needed some outlet for their anger and frustration. Somewhere along the line the group lost its ability to think rationally and each person became a part of a mindless mob. For some reason this propelled me to listen to my mother who had long been begging me to attend church ever since I can remember. It was there that I met a preacher who preached a loving God, a God who cares about us. A God who watches over us and gives us the strength to bear what we are asked to bear. I felt filled with the love of God and Christ. My understanding of my particular lot in life was deepened and given purpose."

Sam stopped. He looked around at this group of young people and knew, deep in his heart, that they needed to hear personal stories, stories that also reflected their trials and challenges. Many warmed to him and kept coming to his Sabbath classes and they grew in size. Ellen often came and sat with the rest of the class, listening to him with pride and awe.

One day he was asked by a member of the congregation whether he would consider publishing some of his speeches. He was so surprised that he didn't take the offer seriously. What could he have to say that someone would want to read, he wondered. Perhaps someday, he thought.

§§§

Soon Sam felt he had put enough money away to get married. He and Ellen wedded one late summer day in 1840. Elymus and James served as witnesses. Hettie Peters, James' mother, stood with Jennie as she beamed at them with pride. It was a joyous day. Jennie was content.

Sam was able to make a good living with his own shop, making shoes using material of the utmost quality. They agreed to continue to put some money aside to save for his further education. After a year Ellen and Sam had their first child in May of 1841. Now they had a real family.

"Oh Ellen! I will work day and night to keep you and Sam Jr. warm and well fed!"

"Oh? And when will you see us then?" Ellen teased. She was as pleased as Sam. Now she could be a mother, hopefully, to many children. Having been an orphan herself she resolved to stay as healthy as possible so she would always be there for her family.

Along with his shoe business, Sam's ministerial work took on great significance. Although he had not formally studied for the ministry yet, he taught many Sabbath classes and spoke out about the injustices against his people.

"We must not be indifferent to the oppression and discrimination of our race. Can we not speak as one voice, one strong voice against the violence perpetrated on those who protest slavery, whether we are White or Black? Can we rise up as one and trample the divide between Black and White? Nowhere else is the color barrier so blatant as here in these United States. It is a fact that cannot be ignored that the colored man labors under difficulties and burdens that no other people do. And yet we remain silent and divided. Inert. As a race can we not stand as one?"

Free Blacks were often the target of an extreme form of violence: men called "blackbirders", often set upon an unsuspecting Black person on the street of a northern city, kidnapping them and selling them into slavery. The southern slave owners felt threatened by the growing anti-slavery movement in the North. They used everything they could think of to keep their right to own slaves. The divide between North and South grew ever wider and was a continuous debate in Congress. The fear the southerners spread in the public sphere made it very difficult for free-Blacks to be safe walking the streets of Philadelphia. Truth was, no one was safe. Even up north the pro-slavery mobs had been attacking the businesses of abolitionists, both Black and White, and burning down their homes and threatening their families.

§§§

Sam longed to be engaged in more soulful work, work that went to the hearts of the people, as well as his own heart. To this end he studied each evening, after helping Ellen with their growing family.

In 1847, in response to a particularly violent clash between the Irish immigrants and the Blacks in his neighborhood, and upon the advice of his friend Elymus Rogers, Sam decided to move his family to Newark, New Jersey and put himself under the care of the Newark Presbytery and Reverend Brinsmead. He had worked diligently for six years and now it was time to listen to the dictates of his heart. Elymus had already become a minister and said he would help Sam towards his ordination in the Presbyterian Church.

His family safely living with him in the suburbs of Newark, Sam continued his study of the Bible and other religious texts in earnest. He studied during the day, did missionary work in the evenings and gave talks on Sunday nights. They now had three more children: Hester Jane, Elizabeth Victoria and little Garret Smith, born that year. Little Sam had died three years before, at the age of three. Heartbroken, Sam and Ellen focused on the two little girls and their second son, keeping them close by and tending to their health as best they could.

"It pains me to say that prejudice against our race is stronger here in Newark than in Philadelphia," Sam said to his wife one evening in their kitchen. "I am afraid we are going to have to swallow our pride when shopping, or even at times walking down the street. It makes me wonder what we were thinking in moving here."

Sam and Ellen were sitting at their round dinner table eating the last bit of greens from their garden. A loaf of freshly baked bread was in the center of the table giving off a tantalizing aroma. Sam was hungry. It was early October and he had just returned from a missionary meeting in nearby Orange. The children were outside playing a last game of hide and seek before going to bed. James had visited the past weekend, bringing with him Sam's mother. He had taught the children a complicated version of hide and seek while Ellen and Jennie baked and cooked in the kitchen.

"I have already seen evidence of that," Ellen agreed, "I am always astounded at the small-mindedness of some people."

Sam nodded. He was proud of his wife. She had a peaceful way about her and was mostly able to keep calm in the face of rude remarks and even outright hostility. They had been married already for seven years and she still made his heart swell with pride. His temper, on the other hand, often flared when he witnessed injustices, or disrespect. He resolved to try harder to keep his feelings tempered.

He cut himself another piece of bread and spread some butter on it.

"I mean, here it may be less dangerous than in Philadelphia, there is less violence, but the pettiness we face is truly dispiriting. I am afraid for our children."

"They are young enough to not notice too much," Ellen assured him, "but I fear for them when they must start school. It's a long walk. Perhaps if we are still here they will have friends to go with."

Sam was silent for a while. He pondered the state of affairs between common folk, Black and White, living on his street, owning the stores where his wife shopped, playing with his children. He felt in his bones that he had to do something to counteract the growing tension between the White tradesman and the Black.

"It is a phenomenon that those of the Celtic race often have no tolerance for the Negro race. It pains me that our relations are so tense and we're segregated in our worship and church services. I'm sure God did not intend this."

Sam's face was serious. He felt powerless to help his people. How could he remain idle when his own people were enslaved, or living in enforced poverty?

"I will be preaching tomorrow," he said to Ellen, "about the evil effects of slavery, of taking a man's freedom and putting him in bondage. I want to wake people up. We cannot afford to sit on the sidelines and allow this situation to continue."

He was afraid she would protest but she said, "You, my dear Sam, must follow the dictates of your heart. You have enough energy for two men and for you to take up the torch for our people is the right thing. I wouldn't have it any other way. I, however, will tend to our children."

"You are my dearest friend!" He took her hand in his and kissed it. "I am fortunate to have such an understanding wife!"

"I will also bring another matter to the attention of the government of New Jersey," he said as he was wiping his mouth on his napkin. "We pay taxes here, do we not?"

"Yes we do, a king's ransom if you ask me!" said Ellen.

"Well, why should we pay taxes if we don't have the right to vote? Wasn't it unfair taxation and no representation that was the cause of the War for Independence? Our people fought in that war, as I've been taught."

"Yes," replied Ellen. "And how will you tell the government this?"

"I will write to the newspaper. If they publish my article others will see it and perhaps that will have an effect." Sam fiercely believed in the power of the written and spoken word.

During Advent Season that year Sam had received a letter from a Congregational church in Pittsfield, Massachusetts, that was looking for a minister. Elymus Rogers, his friend from the Gerrit Smith School, had suggested him to the search committee. He had passed a preliminary examination in New Jersey that gave him a license to preach but he still needed to be ordained. The Second Congregational Church in Pittsfield, a church established specifically by the Black population, was eager to have its own Black minister. The congregation maintained that they would take the responsibility of getting him ordained.

*Samuel Harrison 1849 before his trip to Massachusetts*

After Christmas Sam started out on his trip to Massachusetts. He was intrigued to be traveling to a "slave free state."

"Did you know Massachusetts was the first state in the Union to make slavery illegal?" Sam asked Ellen as he was readying himself for the trip. "They've been free for a long time now, I think since 1783."

"Where did you find that out?" asked Ellen.

"I heard the story from Elymus. He's been to Pittsfield a few times already. He said that in 1781 a young enslaved woman from the town of Sheffield, in Berkshire County, sued her owner, Colonel Ashley, for her freedom and she won the case with the help of a young lawyer, a Mr. Sedgwick."

"But how did that make Massachusetts a free state?" asked Ellen.

"Well, I don't remember everything Elymus said but I do know that she based her case on a law, I think it was the Massachusetts Constitution that was made law in 1780. It states that "all men are created free and equal." It had never been done before."

"Well, that was foresightful of her! Why doesn't that work for our U.S. Constitution, I wonder?" said Ellen half seriously.

"I'll say," said Sam.

Sitting on the train as it wended its way north along the New York border Sam mused on what it would be like to live in a place like Massachusetts, a true northern state. "I've been emancipated since I was three. I never knew the bonds of slavery, and yet, I think I would feel different living up there. Would I feel safer? Do I fear the new Fugitive Slave Law being debated in Congress? Can I contemplate the idea that I might be taken from the streets of Newark and sold down the river? And separated from my family? Will I be judged by the color of my skin in Massachusetts? Or will I be known and judged for who I am?"

Such were the thoughts passing through Sam's mind on his way north. Pittsfield was a bucolic town surrounded by the rounded hills of Berkshire County. Sam breathed in the cold, fresh air as he approached the home of Dr. John Todd, minister of the white First Congregational Church. It was here he was to meet Mr. Newton, a banker, who, with Dr. Todd, would be the first to interview him for the position as minister of the Second Congregational Church. He presented three letters of recommendation, one from Reverend Dr. Brinsmeade, another from Elymus Rogers, the third from Reverend Condit. They all three knew Dr. Todd from a previous association.

"We have read the letters from the Reverends Brinsmeade and Condit," said Dr. Todd. "You know Rev. Brinsmeade was pastor at this church before I was? And, of course, Elymus

Rogers with whom we are well acquainted. It is good to finally meet you, Mr. Harrison. You come highly recommended."

"It is good to be here!" said Sam.

"I take it your journey was agreeable, Mr. Harrison?" inquired Mr. Newton.

"It was uneventful. I saw much out the train window. And your city is quite pleasant."

"Glad to hear it! We think so. You will be staying with Mrs. Gray on First Street for the length of your visit. We will take you there once we are done here," said Dr. Todd.

After leading him into the parlor they sat down on three upright ladder-back chairs.

"Now for some questions," said Mr. Newton. "How far along are you in your studies?"

"I have finished all the required reading to become a minister," said Sam, "and I am licensed to preach the Gospel. I still must be ordained."

"Well," replied Mr. Newton, "I don't think that will be a problem. We have ministers here who can see to it that you are ordained. And also a Berkshire Association of Congregational Ministers who can help in your preparation. The Congregationalists and the Presbyterians are like-minded enough for you to be ordained in the Congregational Church."

"The Reverend Henry Highland Garnet comes here often from Troy of a Sunday to preach. He has all the qualities needed to prepare you for ordination," agreed Dr. Todd.

"That would work well for me," said Sam. "I would be honored to be given the responsibility of this congregation. I feel I am ready to take this on."

"It would be good to have a man of your abilities and your education within the Congregational Church to help cultivate and tend to the size of this congregation," said Mr. Newton.

Sam looked at the two men. He was full of questions but felt hesitant to voice them. These men were from the First Congregational Church, an all-white church that had recently declined the attendance of colored people. Would he have autonomy to conduct his churchly duties in his own way? Why were they interviewing him without any of his prospective congregation present? Who had founded the Second Congregational Church and why? Although he was profoundly moved to be coming to a place where he would have his own church, working with his own people, he needed more assurance that his family would be welcome and the church could support him.

As though reading his thoughts Mr. Newton asked, "And your family, Mr. Harrison? You have a wife and children, do you not?"

"Yes, my wife Ellen and I have three children."

"We will have to find you larger lodgings, then. We thought this might be the case and can be prepared for that," said Mr. Newton.

"And what about the congregation? I have been in communication with a Mr. Potter who has made contact with me. I assume I will be meeting with him, as well?"

"Why yes, of course. I gather from Mr. Potter you will be meeting tomorrow, and preaching on Sunday. There will be a gathering with the whole congregation afterwards. After all, they are the ones requesting you as minister!" exclaimed Dr. Todd.

"We know it will be tough financially for such a small congregation, at least initially, but our church has committed to be of assistance for the first year," added Mr. Newton.

They looked at Sam expectantly. He met their gaze. He realized they were assessing his willingness to come to Pittsfield as a Congregational minister.

"The committee of the Second Church will make the final decision," said Dr. Todd. "We hope they come to a favorable conclusion!"

After confirming his meeting with the founding members of the congregation the next day, they walked him to Mrs. Gray's boarding house on First Street where he had a warm meal and went to bed, quite eager to be taking the first steps towards ministering to his own congregation and towards ordination.

The next day he met with eight members of the Second Congregational Church on First Street. As he looked around the church, which obviously would need some repairs, he asked why they had separated from the First Congregational Church.

"We had a hankering for our own space," replied Morris Potter, one of the eight committee members. "The Wesleyan Methodist Church building was unoccupied at the time and so we saw an opportunity for our own church. With a little work we thought the church structure would be just what we needed and that we would be prudent to take the chance."

"We have had wonderful temporary ministers preaching to us in the meantime, but now we want our own minister," said Mary Richards.

"Henry Highland Garnet has inspired us no end but now we want a minister of our own," agreed Catharine Fields. "Just between us, we felt unwanted every time we entered the First Congregational church."

Sam felt a tinge of despair. It was not all that different

in a "slave-free" state, he thought. Dismayed but happy to hopefully be able to make things better, he finished the conversation, and making arrangements to preach the next day, he went back to his lodgings to prepare his sermons.

On Sunday the church was modestly filled. Morris Potter said it was the greatest number of people he had seen since the two churches had separated. Sam's reputation as a passionate preacher with a way with words had clearly preceded him. He spoke gently and more generally than usual, respecting that he was new and did not yet know their mettle.

After returning home to his family Sam received a letter from the committee of the Second Congregational Church that they would like to have him come to be their first permanent minister. They could offer him $275 a year plus moving costs.

And so it was set. He would bring his family up the first week in January of 1850. He would be 32 years old in a few months.

*Samuel Harrison and his dear wife Ellen Rhodes Harrison*
from the Family Bible

# Chapter 4

The weather was cold and snowing when they reached Pittsfield on that day in January. For the time being the family had been provided lodgings two miles from the church. The house was small but snug against the winter winds. And, within a week, they were settled in. Baby Alice, almost a year old, seemed strong and healthy. Despite the cold, Ellen was happy in their new town. She hadn't had much time to get about but she liked what she saw. The elm tree in Park Square was massive and gave a feeling of strength and endurance. The people she met were friendly enough. The shops had an abundance of goods. Pittsfield looked well kept, cleaner certainly than Newark, and quite a bit smaller. Some of the houses in the neighborhood of the church were grand and imposing with wide front porches and large gardens. Their house, however, was not in one of those neighborhoods.

"I think this has been a good move," Ellen was saying to Sam, as she unpacked her shopping basket. He was late and she was concerned with the amount of traveling he had to do to function as the new permanent minister of his congregation.

"Although we will have to find a place nearer the church to

53

live if you are to be available to your parishioners, Sam," Ellen remarked. "Especially in such cold and snowy conditions it will be hard for you to tend to the people of this church when they are in need of you if you live such a distance from the church. You travel everywhere on foot, Sam! It makes no sense to be so far away."

Sam looked at Ellen in surprise. He hadn't thought of that. She was always so practical. "I promise I will look into that, dear-heart," he replied. "I will ask the committee if they know of something nearer."

And by spring of that year they had moved into a rental on Third Street, a few blocks from the church.

By the end of May Sam and Ellen had planted a garden to supplement his income. Despite the warm welcome Sam had received, there was little money to pay him a living wage. On occasion he spent time on the shoe bench practicing his trade, making shoes for the people of Pittsfield to earn the extra he needed to feed his growing family. The First Congregational Church which had first paid to bring Sam to Pittsfield had a large treasury and ample funds to pay their ministers well. But his church, the Second Congregational Church was much poorer. When he had first arrived there were eight regularly attending members of the congregation although at the time there were 258 Black residents of the city. One time he asked a member of the congregation why they had split off from the larger church and to his dismay had been told: "We were not welcome to drink from the same communion cup as the Whites" among other indignities and so they decided to break off and establish their own church. They were still connected to the First Congregational Church in some ways, but clearly not financially. This was an unexpected hardship that was never really resolved.

As anticipated, Sam was an engaging and inspiring preacher. Before long his congregation had swelled to include many more of the city residents. By June he had fulfilled the requirements for ordination and was ordained that summer in Williamstown by the Berkshire Association of Congregational Ministers, Elymus Rogers officiating.

After the ordination Sam heard a surprising story. Sitting with Ellen that evening he recounted it to her. "And so I heard from Elymus that his ancestors were brought to this country on a slave ship that foundered off the coast of Connecticut and was shipwrecked. His ancestors were saved and sold to the ancestors of Dr. Todd, who held them in slavery until 1783 when Massachusetts made it illegal to own slaves. That's how Elymus knows Dr. Todd. Isn't that the strangest thing?" Sam sat musing as Ellen cleared the plates.

"The strangest things are often the truest," she said. "Elymus never told you that story before?"

"No," said Sam. "And we spent much time together. He probably didn't think of it." Sam sat quietly for a moment, then continued, "he also told me more of the story of how Massachusetts ended slavery. He said that after that woman I told you about received her freedom she changed her name to Elizabeth Freeman, but everyone called her Mumbet."

"I like that name!" said Ellen. "Mumbet! It has a ring to it."

Sam smiled and continued. "Based on her case, and one other which was brought by a man called Quok Walker in the Worcester area, Massachusetts banned slavery by judicial decree in 1783. So it wasn't an act of the legislature, it was a court decision. It wasn't advertised well; it just kind of happened. So a person pretty much had to hear about it somehow and then tell the man who "owned" him that he was free! But one way or another it worked. By the 1790 census, there were no more slaves listed in Massachusetts. And Mumbet lived to the ripe old age of eighty-five, a legend in Berkshire County."

"As well she should be! Imagine being of such stature as to have the courage to do that! My, my!"

Sam sat back on his chair thinking about the strange ways of the world. He knew that New York state had also banned slavery in 1827, but in a different manner. But here in Massachusetts there had been sixty-five years of freedom. The population of Blacks was pretty small though. "We are still strangers here, strange to people who don't have much exposure to people of a darker hue," he thought. And that hurt the cause because unfamiliarity breeds a fear of the unknown that he and Ellen still felt on the streets of Pittsfield even though it was a free state.

*The Second Congregational Church in Pittsfield as it was then*

# Chapter 5

Sam's confidence in his sermons grew and soon he was able to spend more time helping his parishioners. Many of them lived on the margins of society and had barely enough to eat. His warm heart and deep concern for their plight brought many to hear his Sunday sermons. He made sure the stove in the church was always fired up and that there was something to eat after each service.

"I will be restrained in my admonitions to my congregation until they know me," said Sam one evening to Ellen. "I want them to feel comfortable with me first, and then I will begin to talk about a revival of nightly meetings to call upon the Lord to enter their hearts. We need a larger number of the citizens of Pittsfield coming each Sunday. The more there are the more likely they will be committed to a religious life. Faith gives you a sense of strength to continue the struggle, to continue to push on. And we all need that."

He instituted the practice of Wednesday night revivals to increase the numbers in the congregation. Elymus Rogers came and helped with the first few, baptizing new members and getting people to commit to participating in church events.

Sam was mindful that his passion for the Bible might burn hotter than it did for many in the congregation. He wanted to nurture their relationship to the church so that it nourished them and gave them true meaning. Faith in the Lord, he believed, helped a person weather the trials of life.

"Life is hard here," he thought. "It's a free state but there *is* segregation and discrimination. It is less overt but nonetheless there is a shunning of the colored folk of the city that is all the more distressing for not being acknowledged." He worried about his children. Ellen did her best to protect them, he knew, but it was still hard.

~

As his reputation grew and countless people came to know of him, including abolitionists and politicians in Boston and New Haven, Connecticut and Rhode Island, he received offers to minister to other congregations in other cities. His congregation, however, would not let him go. He was considered an outspoken abolitionist at that time and was known and respected in the anti-slavery world. He both held and attended many abolitionist meetings and heard all the influential traveling lecturers speaking on the subject. He tirelessly read *The North Star,* the weekly paper written by the ex-slave Frederick Douglass in Rochester, New York, promoting abolitionism, African American rights and women's rights and spoke out against slavery in every place he could find an audience.

~

"My fellow citizens of Berkshire County," Sam said to his congregation one Sunday morning. "Can we not have the self-determination to defy the southern states in their enactment of the Fugitive Slave Law? Can we, a small group of people in a small New England town, help our brethren in the South? I say we form a group that will chase out any slave catchers seen in Berkshire county who have come with the intention to retrieve men or women who have escaped their "masters."

Sam looked out over the congregation and saw many a nodding head. Encouraged, he continued. "If we keep our eyes open for white brute-looking men we might be as successful as those who saved Shadrach Minkins in Boston!"

Some of his congregation looked puzzled. Who was Shadrach Minkins?

"Shadrach Minkins was a man born on a slave plantation in Norfolk, Virginia," continued Sam. "At about the age of thirty he escaped and made his way to Boston. A few months after his arrival he was caught by a slave catcher. But a group of people who were trained to keep their eyes open for such things, saw what was going on and thwarted his capture. It was a dramatic event in which nearly 200 people snuck him out of the courtroom where the slave catcher was proclaiming his right to take him back to Virginia. Within minutes Shadrach was spirited away and set on his way to Canada." Sam was inspired to try and do something for his people other than talks and pamphlets. "Can we be as watchful and full of initiative? I think so!"

And so a group was formed with the intention of thwarting any "blackbirders" or slave catchers.

~

"Mama, Mama, come quickly!" called Hester Jane, just nine years old. "Mama come. Alice is burning hot and she won't open her eyes."

Ellen, who had put them to bed an hour ago, bounded up the stairs, clutching her apron and skirts in her hand. As she entered the tiny bedroom that Hester Jane shared with her brother and sister she saw little Alice, who was almost two, begin to shudder as she lay in the crumpled bed clothes. "I've tried cooling her with this cloth, Mama but I don't think it's helping." Hester was in tears.

Ellen sat on the edge of the bed and reached for Alice. Her little body was indeed burning hot.

"Hester, don't worry, you did all you could. Go downstairs and ask your father to get some vinegar mixed with cool water in a bowl with some clean cloths. Bring it up here. We will cool little Alice down."

Hester did as she was told while Ellen removed some of Alice's clothing. It was February and she was dressed in many layers of wool. The upstairs bedrooms were cold in the winter so she was careful to protect Alice from drafts.

Sam came up the stairs with the cooling vinegar water and sat beside Hester and Garret as Ellen wrapped strips of cloth soaked in the vinegar water around Alice's legs to bring the fever down. They rubbed eucalyptus ointment on her chest and dribbled cool chamomile tea on her feverish lips. Ellen held her close as she touched her lips to her forehead to feel her fever.

"Mama, what can we do?" asked Hester.

Ellen was silent for a moment. "We can love her. I don't know what else can be done. We'll keep cooling her down but this fever has taken powerful hold of our little girl." She hiccoughed as she tried to keep her tears at bay. It would not do to cry in front of the children.

Ellen nudged Sam to take Alice in his arms so that she could comfort Hester and Garret and urge them to lie down to sleep.

Around two o'clock that morning, Ellen felt a change in her daughter. The other two were asleep, as was Sam, all lying together in the bed. Ellen was holding Alice while resting her own head against the bedstead. She looked down at Alice's face and saw a peacefulness come over daughter. She nudged Sam to wake up. "I think her fever has broken," she said. Sam smiled and looked relieved. He lay back down only to sit bolt upright when he heard Ellen let out a sob. "What is it? What is it?" he cried out. He looked at Alice and then at Ellen and knew that little Alice was breathing her last breaths. They both had seen the look too many times before and knew they had lost another child. With an unfathomable sense of loss the two of them rocked her little body in their arms until the sun rose. When it was fully light they woke Hester and Garret.

"Hester, Garret, come here. Come into my arms." Sam said to them. Hester's frightened face told Sam she knew. "Where is Alice?" she cried. "Where is Alice?"

"Your sister has gone to her heavenly father," explained Sam. "I am so, so sorry." He gazed at his two children and saw such anguish. How could he make them feel better? "Please little Hester, please Garret, know that she is at peace."

Hester looked wild-eyed at her parents. "No, Mama, no!" she cried out in fear. "Mama, it's not true!"

Ellen held the two children close to her heart as they sobbed. After a while she gently disengaged their arms and said, "Come, children, come and say goodbye." She led them downstairs and into the front room where Sam had carried Alice and placed her on a wooden table.

The children looked at their sister uncomprehendingly. How could this be the little girl they had played with yesterday? Where had she gone? She was so still and waxen. Who would play with her? Hester hesitantly went up to her sister to touch her face. "Did I do this, Mama?" she cried out in pain.

"Precious girl! Alice died of a fever. You are not to blame." Ellen was startled that Hester would consider such a thing. Thinking quickly she said, "Help me get her dressed, Hester! She needs to look her prettiest as she goes to heaven." Hester let out a wail but was willing to be guided upstairs to choose Alice's clothing. She selected a rose colored dress and pinafore with a bonnet of white cambric and fine wool stockings. They dressed her carefully, anointed her face and hands with lavender oil, put her quilt over her and sat around the table and wept.

The house was silent for most of the day. Some of the congregation came bringing casserole dishes and pies. No one had much to say. They had mostly all suffered the same kind of loss and knew the pain the family was feeling. Two days later, on a blustery February morning, she was laid to rest in a tiny coffin in the Pittsfield Cemetery.

§§§

In March Ellen discovered she was pregnant again. Her heart leapt a little bit in her chest as she told Sam. It helped ease the ache that was constantly present. Little Ellen was born in October of that year.

Sam and Ellen had five more children during the next eight years: Urania, Mary, Lavinia, Samuel and George. To their profound anguish Urania, Lavinia and Samuel each died soon after birth. Both Ellen and Sam were heartbroken again and again. They took great comfort in each other and their surviving children. Never far from feeling the weight of their loss, they learned to take nothing for granted. Each life was precious. They had five remaining children to keep their hearts open and loving: Hester Jane, Garret, little Ellen, Mary, and George. And so it stayed until Henry, who also died in infancy, and finally Lydia joined the family 1861. Lydia was their last child.

After years of renting, Sam realized it was more economical to own his own home. Early on he had purchased a piece of land on Third Street which had remained an empty lot where Ellen had planted her garden for many a year. Now, after six years, it was time to get his house built. He knew the First Congregational Church had great wealth and went to visit Dr. Todd to borrow a sum of about $300. Dr. Todd responded that while there was wealth in the church it was not sanctified. This curious statement was a setback but after much thought, Sam approached an abolitionist colleague, the former Governor of Massachusetts, Governor George Briggs, and a few of his abolitionist friends to borrow enough money to build his house for his family. By 1857 they were living in their own home, much to his and Ellen's relief. Now she could tend her garden, raise chickens and a pig and grow enough food to feed the family. They needed to supplement what Sam earned. She also took in sewing jobs from her neighbors and members of the congregation. Her nimble fingers mended and stitched each garment sent her way. Eventually Hester Jane and little Ellen were able helpers.

With their new house to live in Sam became aware of the dilapidated state of his church. He urged the congregation to try and raise half the funds to renovate the church and he would raise the rest.

"And how are we supposed to do that?" inquired a member of the congregation.

"Why, I think we'll have to hold a Christmas bazaar! We

can all make things can we not?" said Ellen.

"Yes, we can do that! The men can make wooden toys and we can bake and make jams and jellies," said another.

"What about also putting on a concert and selling tickets?" asked Hester Jane who loved to sing.

"That we can do!" said Ellen. "Let's ask Mr. Newton's friend, George Root, if he will help us get one together. He has a choir in Boston but often comes here to direct 'community sings' so we can all learn new songs."

And so it was done. Within less than a year they had a cozy new church with new pews, stabilized walls, a new floor and windows and a wonderful coal stove to heat the church in the winter. News of their success traveled fast! Churches in Troy, New York; Portland, Maine and Hartford, Connecticut, all invited him to relocate to their cities. His congregation, however, again refused to let him go. And secretly he was pleased to remain in Pittsfield, the city that had first welcomed him into their midst. He felt at home there.

~

Sam was addressing his congregation on a cold winter Sunday. They knew him well now, and trusted his take on matters of the world. He felt he could speak freely about what was troubling him. And it was the unchanging conditions of inequality and discrimination that his people continued to experience that was concerning him. He looked down from his pulpit. As the west was opening up and new territories were looking to become states there was always that troublesome question—whether they should be slave states or Free Soil states. Congress had said it was not a matter for Congress to determine. Each new state should have the "liberty" to decide for themselves. Thus the Kansas-Nebraska Act was passed.

These two new states, Kansas and Nebraska, would decide for themselves.

"We should take no half measures in our fight for freedom and equality. The lives of colored men have always been cheap in the South... This new act of Congress, the Kansas-Nebraska Act, is a prime example of misunderstanding the ways of men. Do we really think that the highest and best of humanity will prevail in this kind of a decision? Do we really think the American people need only to be educated about the devastating effects of human slavery ... to understand it must be abolished ...? I only wish it were so."

Even to Sam his words fell flat. He felt no fire today. He was tired. He was cold. In fact, he was also hungry. With such a low salary he and Ellen often rationed their portion of food so that the children would not go hungry. He felt he was talking against a tide of inertia that sapped his strength. He wanted to fight for the emancipation of all slaves. He wanted everyone north and south to be free and able to work for their own living. But he was tired. It was too much of a struggle. And he could see his congregation was feeling the same way. He drew his sermon to a close. Looking down at his people he said:

"Let's gather in the community room and drink the hot cider and share our food. We all could use some warmth and fellowship."

# Chapter 6

"Ellen? Ellen? Are you home?" Sam came rushing into the house on Third Street. "Ellen! I have the most wonderful news!"

"Sam? I'm upstairs. Can it wait until I come down?" called Ellen from their bedroom.

"I'm coming up," called Sam. "I just cannot wait!"

He bounded up the stairs and gathered Ellen into his arms. "I'm eager to tell you this because it helps ease all the burdens of my soul. You know how weighed down I've been, dear-heart."

Ellen extracted herself from his arms and looked him deeply in the eyes. She knew how troubled he had been, for how long his sermons had carried the heavy weight of urging his people to get up and fight against the injustices hurled at the citizens of a darker hue, all across the Union. She knew his fiery spirit was tamped down, almost unable to be ignited again. He urged his congregation to speak out against the enslavement of his people. But they were all—afraid. Afraid of being the target themselves of violence and discrimination. Afraid of losing their homes or even their lives to racial mobs.

They seemed paralyzed with fear. And he himself had begun to feel desperate. It was all just too great a burden ...

"I know dear. And I am thrilled to hear anything that brings back the light to your eyes." She smiled at him, feeling encouraged and buoyant.

"Well then, this is what it is: next Thursday evening our own Frederick Douglass is coming to Pittsfield. He'll be speaking at Community Hall at 7:30. I want us to go!"

Ellen looked at her husband. "I am so happy. I'm so, so pleased. I'd love to come with you! Hester Jane can care for the children for the evening. I'll prepare supper beforehand and make sure all is ready for their bedtime ..." she tripped over her words in her eagerness to see the light in Sam's eyes continue to shine.

Sam's face was alight: "I'll visit each household if need be to insist that each member of our congregation come and be inspired. Inspired to have hope again, hope that we can all join together and make slavery a sad historical fact rather than the law of the land. Reverend Rogers will be there. I will invite Dr. Todd."

"Yes, yes dear. Let's lose no time in gathering a crowd that will fill the hall with both Black and White."

Ellen and Sam went downstairs and gathered their children together to help with the evening meal. Hester Jane looked at her parents: "What are we celebrating? Is this some anniversary I have forgotten?" she asked.

Ellen shook her head: "No dear, we're just happy to have your father back. He's full of enthusiasm for life again."

Thursday evening came and the hall was crowded to the rafters. The upper gallery was reserved for the Black residents of the county while the White residents sat below. The crowd was made up equally of men and women. Never before had Pittsfield seen so many men and women gathered together under one roof. The sound of the multitude hummed with excitement. Frederick Douglass, born a slave in Baltimore, Maryland and author of the famous book: *Narrative of the Life of Frederick Douglass, by Himself* was by now one of the most famous men in America. He was known for his impassioned speeches on abolition, on social justice, temperance and the rights of women. Since the 1820s former slaves and freed slaves had been writing 'narratives' or accounts of what it had been like to be a slave, to break free, and then to become a part of the abolition movement. Indeed, not a few had been murdered for their outspokenness against slavery. But none had touched the heart of the nation as deeply as Frederick Douglass. To hear him speak was to have your heart wrung out, to feel your bones rattle in harmony with his words. Sam knew this and he wanted his people in Pittsfield to be roused out of their timid inactivity and to hop on the railway-train of abolition, to feel their own power to change the world and change the course of history. He felt that all they needed was to be inspired.

A hush fell over the crowd as Mr. Douglass climbed to the stage. An inspiring figure with broad brow and welcoming smile, his piercing eyes surveyed the crowd. They softened as he saw the number of women present. He looked upward at the crowded gallery, at all the people standing there. Sam thought he caught his eye. He certainly smiled at Ellen! Then he cleared his throat.

"I am here this evening straight from Rochester, New York, where I now live. I have with me 1,000 copies of my newspaper *The North Star*. It is the instrument I use mostly to publicize the causes of abolition, temperance and women's rights. Tonight I am promoting my newspaper because in it I claim that the Constitution of the United States, which was inaugurated almost 100 years ago, to 'form a more perfect union, establish justice, insure domestic tranquility, provide for common defense, promote the general welfare, and secure the blessings of liberty ...' could not well have been designed at the same time to maintain and perpetuate a system of plunder and murder like slavery, especially as not one word can be found in the Constitution to authorize such a belief ..."

The audience was electrified. Mr. Douglass was speaking with such authority about a revered document that governed the lives of *all* the citizens of the United States. And he was saying that the Constitution did not sanction slavery. Sam leaned in and listened with a glad heart. Occasionally he looked at Ellen to see how she was responding to Mr. Douglass's inspiring words. After one of his glances she took his hand and squeezed it. He leaned over to her and whispered, "If this doesn't rouse the people of Pittsfield to be more outspoken I don't know what will!" She smiled in agreement. It was 1861 and talk of a war between the states was getting louder and more insistent. She knew her husband was firing up to take a lead in the discussions and use every means he had to promote the cause of freedom for their people.

"If there is no struggle, there is no progress. We must fight to destroy slavery. I am calling for a war of abolition. Ours is only one humble voice, but such as it is, we give it freely to our country." Mr. Douglass's voice rose above the murmurings of the crowd, calling out in agreement ... "A war undertaken and brazenly carried on for the perpetual enslavement of colored men, calls logically and loudly for colored men to help suppress it ..." Mr. Douglass looked out at the crowd.

"Can anyone tell us why this should not be an abolition war?"

Sam looked around. Each person's eyes were fixed on Mr. Douglass. No one was fidgeting, no one was looking around. Everyone was enthralled, eagerly hanging on his every word.

"Have we not a right here?" Mr. Douglass's voice had gotten quiet. "For 300 years or more, we have had a foothold on this continent. We have grown up with you. Our hands removed the stumps from your fields and raised the first crops and brought the first produce to your tables. We have fought for this country ... I consider it settled that the Black and White people of America ought to share a common destiny. The White and Black must fall or flourish together. We have been with you, are still with you, and mean to be with you to the end. We shall neither die out nor be driven out. But we shall go with you and stand either as a testimony against you or as evidence in your favor throughout your generations." Here he was speaking primarily to the white audience. The crowd was transfixed. No one spoke with that kind of authority to Blacks and Whites together.

The crowd rose as one and cheered and stomped. They could not have enough of this man's words, so true they rang out, so true they were hanging there in the air as the listeners gathered eagerly around Mr. Douglass, impatient to buy his newspaper and read his inspiring and encouraging words for themselves.

"We have been roused! We had been inspired," Sam exclaimed to Ellen. "Now, *now* there will be no more paralysis! We'll work with this man in the cause of freedom and equality. Now we shall join with him to help end slavery."

That Sunday, Sam stepped up to his pulpit and spoke to his congregation with renewed vigor.

"My fellow citizens! Since the founding of this country we have been here working side by side with the first people to emigrate from Europe. For, if you remember, the year before the Mayflower landed the Puritans on Plymouth Rock, a cargo of African enslaved men and women landed in Jamestown, Virginia, which is over 240 years ago. All these long years we have toiled for the benefit of others. Is it not time to claim our personhood? Our humanity? Our rights as human beings?"

The people listened, nodding their heads in agreement, shouting out on occasion that they had been moved. The atmosphere was different, there was an encouraging change coming about, they could feel it in the air.

"As your previous minister, Rev. Henry Highland Garnet, has so eloquently spoken to you, 'Think of the undying glory that hangs around the ancient name of Africa and forget not that you are native born American citizens, and as such you are justly entitled to all the rights that are granted to the freest.' I echo these words, dear friends, and so must you. Take them into your heart and make them your own!"

~

The congregation seemed to take heart. Events were moving in the right direction. Momentum was becoming an unstoppable force. Later that day he reflected on the events that had led up to this new spirit of optimism.

Elymus Rogers had come for his yearly visit to Pittsfield. He had many friends and acquaintances in the Berkshires and looked forward to the discussions that often erupted on his visits.

"And what about the Free Soil Party now being called the

"Republican" Party? Does that not make it more inclusive of other ways of thinking? The name "Free Soil" brands you as a believer in abolition. Now with this neutral name, anyone can choose to become a member!" Elymus said to Sam as they were sitting with two friends, Mr. Hubbard and Mr. Mitchell one summer evening.

"Yes," Sam agreed, "I think it was a politically smart move to unite and rename the Republican party. It can now distance itself from the credo: "Free Soil, Free Speech, Free Labor, Free Men." Opposition to the expansion of slavery isn't so obvious anymore. An unthinking, unsuspecting southerner could ostensibly join, no?"

Elymus laughed, "you don't think that would happen do you? Not in the South, anyway. But those new settlers in Kansas and Nebraska could be excused for missing the Republican Party's mission! The word "Republican" doesn't imply abolitionism or free speech. We can only hope enough men join and vote to ban the expansion of slavery into those two territories."

"There is enough talk of voter fraud and intimidation to have grave concerns," said Mr. Mitchell. "Rich slave owners are moving west and buying up the best land for themselves. Then they use their slave labor to develop it. The free farmers you're talking about are left with poor land and only themselves and hired labor to work it. It's a travesty."

"Not even the likes of our own Senator Charles Sumner have had much of an effect on how this issue progresses," said Mr. Hubbard. "He has recovered enough now to return to Congress." [Mr. Hubbard was referring to the beating Massachusetts Senator Sumner had received from a southern Congressman after giving his famous anti-slavery speech

*"The Crime Against Kansas" three years before. He had used strong language to describe Senator Stephen A. Douglas of Illinois as a "Squire of Slavery." Douglas was the sponsor of the Kansas-Nebraska Act which sought to allow the new states in the west to decide by vote whether to be a slave-free state or one that allowed slavery. The southerners had taken offense and one of the Congressmen had beaten Senator Sumner so severely on the Senate floor that Sumner had had to take almost three years to recover from his injuries. The beating, as well as the Kansas-Nebraska Act were heated and much debated topics everywhere.]*

"It is frightening, nay terrifying, to see how the pro-slavery advocates are terrorizing the rest of Kansas," said Sam. "They are trying to intimidate the entire state into voting to allow slavery. As if that kind of tactic would work with a man who truly sees the cruelty of chattel slavery."

"I hear they are burning homes and kidnapping husbands and fathers, torturing families, destroying crops, even murdering people in an effort to intimidate," replied Elymus. "It is a terrifying subject that incites passionate emotions. John Brown has been speaking in cities and towns to raise money to fight these pro-slavery thugs."

"Frederick Douglass said of John Brown that *'although he is a White gentleman, he is in sympathy a Black man,'* said Sam. "I know this to be the case; he is a man of action. He fights a Holy War against slavery. But he gets little financial support from our community. I am not sure what I think of that. Do we sit passively by as these settlers destroy the farms of the free-soilers or do we advocate a violent response? I truly do not know."

After a pause Sam added, "I am not aware that John Brown

is inciting violence as much as he is trying to make us responsive to the need to resist the expansion of slavery into the western states. He is a man of God who is often described as a man prone to violence. I think this is inflammatory propaganda on the part of the rich and powerful men of the South. They have such a tight hold on how the situation is portrayed to the rest of the country, that we all are led to believe John Brown is impractical and even unhinged. I think he is not."

The men were silent as they contemplated the unlawful brutality of what was going on in the West.

§§§

In October of the year 1859, John Brown and twenty-two volunteer followers, including seventeen white men, three free Blacks and two slaves, raided the United States arsenal at Harper's Ferry, Virginia to obtain enough weapons to arm slaves to fight the slave-owning settlers in Kansas. It was not successful. Robert E. Lee, a U.S. Marines colonel, responded at the behest of President Buchanan a few days later and was able to defeat the men. Ten men were killed, seven captured and five escaped, only to be captured at a later date. John Brown and four others were hanged as traitors. It was the last of the twenty-one slave rebellions that had begun in the year 1526 and resulted eventually in the Civil War. Before the attack on the Harper's Ferry arsenal many workers Black and White had banded together to fight oppression and unfair labor practices. The South felt it was just this kind of solidarity between Black and White laborers that made John Brown's attack almost a success. The politicians in the South realized they would have to mobilize to destroy the feeling of unity between Black and White laborers and create dissent among them if the South was to preserve its right to "own" slaves. It made the claim that banning slavery in the new territories was unconstitutional. Any unity between Blacks and Whites was a threat to slavery. Therefore that unity must be destroyed.

~

During the presidential election of 1860, Abraham Lincoln, who belonged to the Republican party, was pitted against John C. Breckinridge, Stephen A. Douglas, and John Bell. Partially because of the quality of Lincoln's oratory in the debates, the new Republican party became a major political force in the North. It created an even greater divide between North and South, between anti-slavery abolitionists and pro-slavery advocates.

During the campaign the South threatened to secede from the Union if a Republican was elected to the White House. It claimed in doing so it wanted to "preserve the Union." This curious phrase remained their refrain throughout the war and after. Lincoln did win the election and became the 16th president of the United States. But, before his inauguration on March 4, 1861, seven slave states seceded from the Union and formed the Confederacy of Southern States: they were South Carolina, Mississippi, Florida, Alabama, Georgia, Louisiana and Texas. President Lincoln had organized a Peace Conference between these southern states and the North, but they were not able to find a compromise. In claiming to want to "preserve the Union," they thrust the thin edge of the wedge of war firmly in place. And so, with heavy hearts both sides began to prepare for war. Over the next three months four more states seceded from the Union: Virginia, Arkansas, North Carolina and Tennessee.

§§§

And then the news came.

At 4:30 a.m. on April 12, 1861, the first shot was fired on Union troops by Confederate troops at Fort Sumter in Charleston, South Carolina. Fort Sumter was an important fortification in the mouth of the Charleston Harbor that had been held by Union troops since April of 1860 in preparation for any type of aggression from the Southern States. The first gun was fired by Confederate troops on the Union soldiers, commanded by Major Robert Anderson, and war was declared. No one knew whether to rejoice or mourn.

# PART II

# Chapter 7

The day was hot and sultry. It was the 31st of July, 1863 and the war had been going on for over two years. The Emancipation Proclamation had been in effect for over seven months. Sam had left the pulpit of the Second Congregational Church to better serve the war effort. He was working for the National Freedmen's Relief Society to solicit aid for freed Blacks of the Sea Islands of South Carolina. It was hard work but it felt good to be directly helping the many freed people who had been fighting for their and his freedom.

It was as hot a summer as anyone could remember. July's skies remained blue every day. Occasionally thunderhead clouds could be seen forming around the peak of Mt. Greylock to the north but no rain had come in weeks. Everything was dry. Ellen was hanging the final bits of laundry on the line in the yard, picking through her basket looking for clothes pins. She was glancing at the sky when Sam came out from the kitchen where he had been looking for something to eat. No tomatoes yet, he thought, but there was a bowl of black raspberries. He remembered that Hester Jane and Mary had been out picking in the morning. He thoughtfully scooped up a handful and went out to speak with Ellen.

"I have been contacted by Governor Andrew, Ellen," Sam reported quietly. "I have here a letter in my hand that asks me to meet his train tomorrow morning at 9:00 a.m. He is coming in from Boston."

"What do you think he wants?"

"It doesn't say, but I am sure it has to do with the dreadful losses of the 54th."

The 54th. The regiment he had so ardently petitioned for. The first regiment of Black soldiers to be raised in the North, 1,007 of them recruited from twenty-four states, fifteen northern, five southern and four border states. Oh, how hard it was to think of how many of those brave men now lay dead so far from home. And their commander, Colonel Robert Gould Shaw, whose wife was from nearby Lenox, also dead, killed in the assault on Fort Wagner.

Sam's heart was full of anguish. He had spent months rousing and recruiting these men to join up. He sat down hard on the bench, his face in his hands. Ellen came and put an arm around his shoulders: "You couldn't have foreseen this, Sam. They knew, they all knew there was a chance they would be killed for the cause."

Sam shook his head back and forth. He knew this, but still he felt deeply responsible.

"They were so young. How can you know what you are getting into when you are eighteen or twenty? We know the families from Berkshire. I helped to recruit them. I said it was an opportunity of a lifetime. I said it was a fight to end slavery, and that it is. But the reality of what I was saying only becomes clear as the lives of the soldiers are lost. And such a short seven weeks later so many of the men of the 54th are gone from us."

Ellen sat next to him, holding his hand. She waited for him to regain his composure. Presently he sighed heavily. "I must go to Eli Franklin's family; he is wounded and there is not much expectation he will live. I will give them our heartfelt condolences. I don't know what else to say." He smiled wearily at Ellen as he heaved himself to his feet and walked to the garden gate. It was a duty of the saddest order. He didn't want to go, but he also didn't want to leave them in the dark.

~

From the time the first shot was fired on April 12, 1861, men of African descent had been petitioning the government for authorization to join the ranks to fight to free their brethren in the South. They had consistently been told "this is a white man's war." But they knew this was a war of abolition, a war to destroy slavery and were determined to play a part in it. There was much public discussion about a Black man's "ability to fight." Fear was expressed in newspapers and periodicals at the image of an army of Black men. Racism and bigotry were expressed publicly and without shame despite the reason for the war. But the announcement of the Preliminary Emancipation Proclamation in September of 1862 and the enormous losses of the Union army put an end to the resistance. It had become a practical matter as well as a moral one. No longer could those in power ignore the willingness of men of African descent to fight in the war. The Emancipation Proclamation had made ending slavery a goal of the war. Not "preserving the Union," now it was openly a war for the abolition of slavery. And they needed the men to swell the ranks of the Union army. It was no longer expedient to ban these men.

The governors of each state were responsible for recruiting Black soldiers. Massachusetts was the first state in the North to raise African American troops for the war. Governor Andrew, an ardent abolitionist and a firm supporter of equality between the races, and Massachusetts Senator Charles Sumner, had been asking for permission from the War Office to form a regiment of Black soldiers for more than a year already. They adamantly expressed their conviction that Black men were capable not only of performing their soldierly duties but also of exercising leadership.

"If Southern slavery should fall, and colored men should have no hand and play no conspicuous part in the task, the result would leave the colored man a mere helot*," Andrew wrote. They would have 'lost their masters, but not found a country.' (*a member of the class of unfree men above slaves owned by the state.)

They advocated for the commission of Black officers as well as troops. After the Emancipation Proclamation was read on January 1st the War Office issued permission for the mustering of Black troops, but no recruitment of Black officers. This was too controversial for the politicians. Governor Andrew bowed to their pressure to exclude Blacks from the officer corps. Advertisements were placed in newspapers asking "Colored Men, Good Men of African Descent" to come and join the regiment being formed in Massachusetts, promising "$100 bounty at the expiration of the term of service and $13 per month and State aid for families." And thus the 54th Massachusetts Volunteer Infantry Regiment (Colored) was formed with White officers and Black troops. Colonel Robert Gould Shaw, a White officer from Boston and "a young man of military experience, of firm Anti-Slavery principles,

ambitious, superior to a vulgar contempt for color, and a faith
in the capacity of Colored men for military service" wrote Gov.
Andrew in a letter, was recruited to command the regiments,
the 54th and the 55th. Each recruit was a man known to
be in good standing in his community, who could read and
write and had demonstrable skills in the workforce. Gov.
Andrew, in choosing these men wanted to show the country
that Black soldiers could fight as well and disciplined as any
White soldier. His project to recruit and train Black soldiers
to fight in the South was carried out with consciousness and
precision and a serious attention to all the details this kind of
undertaking entailed.

~

In February of that year, a month after the Emancipation
Proclamation, Sam had been asked to help recruit Berkshire
men to join up to fight this war to free the slaves.

"I have been instructed by Governor Andrew and the War
Office," Sam had said "to assure you that you will receive
equal pay, equal treatment and equal benefits as the White
soldiers."

He was speaking to a group of men who had responded to
the ads that had been tacked up all over Berkshire County.

"Even so, it's hard to know what to do, Sir," said Levi
Jackson, a young man from Great Barrington. "We've heard
some news of what it is like down there in the South."

"Yes, we've heard tell that if we, as Black soldiers, are
captured by the Confederates we will most surely be enslaved,
or worse yet, shot," said Henry Burghardt from Lee.

Sam had also heard first hand of the carnage on the
battlefields, especially the danger to Black prisoners. It was
no secret. And yet, there were so many reasons to go.

*Recruitment Broadside plastered all across the North*

"We have heard many things, men, and they may or may not be accurate. We can only hope and pray they are not," he said.

"Do you remember the words of Frederick Douglass?" Sam had asked Eli Franklin who was a member of Sam's congregation. "Remember the fire we felt when he spoke of a war of abolition? This is that war! This is the war we have been eager for. A chance to right this horrible wrong. A chance to be an active agent of freedom. Remember how it felt to imagine we could do something about our predicament?"

Eli had nodded and looked around at the rest of the men. A few of them had been at the evening with Frederick Douglass.

"And Mr. Douglass's sons, Lewis and Charles, have joined up, as well," Sam had continued. "They will be with you in your regiment, I presume. And remember, you will be paid a fair and equal wage, as well as a bounty for signing up."

This had been a selling point for many of the men who were worried about their families and how they would manage without them. It was a serious consideration to decide to enlist in an army that was fighting so far from home and with so little certainty as to the outcome. Nevertheless many signed up. The promise of equal pay and the $100 bounty were enough to counter their fear of reprisal.

That evening Sam pondered the fact that their president, Abraham Lincoln, had spoken severely to his constituents in the North. The President saw that many of the White Americans in the supposedly liberal North did not want to fight to free Black Americans but that Black Americans seemed willing to fight for them. He remonstrated with these "Copperheads," as they were known, that if they wouldn't fight to free the Negro then they should fight to preserve the Union. Sam gladdened to the fact that Lincoln seemed unwavering in his intention to keep his promise to free the slaves. It made recruitment feel more honest and substantial.

The 54th and 55th Regiments had trained at Fort Meigs in Readville outside of Boston under Colonel Robert Gould Shaw and Colonel Norbert Hallowell for two months. Much attention was given by the press to all aspects of the Regiments, their training, their camp, their men. Finally they could proclaim that the war was about slavery and that these men were going to contribute to the emancipation of their race. How they trained, how they conducted themselves, who they were, was fiercely debated and reported. It was a favorite topic of conversation that spring throughout New England and beyond, although not all were in favor of arming Black men. "Every race has fought for Liberty and its own progress," Governor Andrew had maintained. "The colored race will create its own future by its own brains, hearts and hands."

Frederick Douglass counseled Lincoln that "once you put upon the black man the blue uniform, once you put upon him the 'U.S.' saying 'United States,' once you put brass buttons on him and a cap and give him a rifle and give him a pistol and make him a soldier of the nation and send him off in battle to defend the nation and also to help preserve the Union, once you have done that, then no power on Earth can deny the full rights of citizenship in due course." And Lincoln realized that to counteract the losses on the Union side the recruitment of Black soliders was a matter of victory or defeat.

Frederick Douglass had written to the soldiers at their training camp in Readville: "We can get at the throat of treason and slavery through the State of Massachusetts. She was first in the war of Independence; first to break the chains of her slaves; first to make the black man equal before the law; first to admit colored children to her common schools. She was the first to answer with her blood the alarm-cry of the nation when its capital was menaced by the Rebels. You know her patriotic Governor, and you know Charles Sumner. I need add no more. Massachusetts now welcomes you as her soldiers.".......

When the 54th and 55th regiments had marched proudly through the streets of Boston on May 28th on their way to the ships that would carry them to Beaufort, South Carolina Sam had looked on with pride and concern. Thousands had turned out to see them off. Sam stood beside Governor Andrew as the parade got under way. Much was being made of these men who were willing to lay down their lives for the Union as well as the destruction of slavery. He had made the journey to Boston on the same train as Annie Haggerty Shaw, Col. Shaw's newlywed wife. She had acknowledged him with a smile and a nod, knowing that Sam had helped recruit men for the 54th Massachusetts Volunteer Infantry. Sam had tipped his hat to her "Good morning Mrs. Shaw" and gone towards the back of the train. He was proud to have been invited to attend this event to see the men off to war, but his heart was nonetheless full of trepidation. And now, now he was to hear more news about these men of the 54th.

*"Private Charles H. Arnum.*

*"Private Abraham F. Brown."*

*"Sergeant Henry F. Steward."*

*"Alexander H. Johnson, Musician"*

*Soldiers of the 54th*

The next morning, August 1, 1863, Sam was at the Pittsfield train station to meet the 9:00 a.m. from Boston. Governor Andrew's train came chugging into the station. The steam from the engine seemed to saturate the air making it even muggier. Sam wiped the sweat from his brow. What could this man want of him, he wondered?

The train lurched to a halt. The governor came down the steps preceded by four men who seemed to be in his entourage, fussing with his luggage and looking at the crowd. One of the men, who knew Sam, signaled him to approach the governor.

"Why Reverend Harrison! I have been hearing such glowing things about you!" were the Governor's first words.

Sam grasped his hand in both of his. "And I the same of you!" he replied.

The governor took Sam's arm and they began walking towards the entrance to the train station. "It is truly good to see you, Reverend Harrison! I've been thinking about you and your work for the 54th."

Sam nodded. He wondered what the Governor was going to ask of him.

"Your speech in Williamstown on *The Cause and Cure for the War* has taken on a life of its own! I have heard more testimonies of its fiery content and, of course, its recommendation for the enlistment of Black troops, than of any other speech in recent memory! Could we dare think that because of your speech President Lincoln has reversed his policy to exclude Black recruits from fighting in this war?"

"Well, I don't know about that!" said Sam. "But I did fiercely recommend Black enlistment in that speech and it was published!" Sam stopped walking and looked the governor in the eyes and continued, "One thing I do know is that our enlisted men are fighting a brave and disciplined fight as we knew they would. No longer can they be described as savages and brutes incapable of following orders." He still burned at the things that had been said to rationalize the barring of Black recruitment. It sickened him.

The governor looked at Sam, standing there so straight and tall. He narrowed his eyes to get a better view of him. "Yes, quite. We knew this would be the case. It's good the world knows it now too."

He paused and then went on, "You know, I also have been a trumpeter of the 54th and 55th regiments." he said thoughtfully. "This is not a White man's war, as many in the South proclaim! This is a war for America, a war between two opposing views of humanity. I for one, am not afraid to proclaim this a war to abolish slavery, a war of abolition, nothing less and nothing more. Freedom for all, finally. Freedom, justice and the chance for a dignified life for every human being on this hallowed earth."

Sam looked at this earnest abolitionist with tremendous respect, and yes, almost love. How grateful he was to him, and how much more grateful he was going to be. He murmured quietly, "Yes, Sir, I do realize the support we have had from you!"

"Well, I do support you fully. Now, as you must have realized, I am here to give our country's condolences to the widow of Colonel Robert Gould Shaw."

Colonel Shaw had married Anna Kneeland Haggerty of the neighboring town of Lenox twenty-six days before taking command of the 54th Massachusetts Voluntary Infantry. Barely two months into his service he had led the July assault on Fort Wagner on Morris Island in South Carolina. It was the first major battle of the war fought by Black troops. As had been reported they had fought a fearless and well-ordered fight, proving their worth as soldiers. But Colonel Shaw had lost his life along with thirty of his troops.

"Yes, I thought that might be the case. I have heard of the many killed at the battle at Fort Wagner. Do we have more deaths?"

"Oh, no, no, none that I have heard of."

"Will you convey my condolences as well? I have had the fortune to have met Mrs. Shaw and would like her to know we are praying for her."

"Yes, I will, of course." The Governor cleared his throat. "Ahem, I am here on another matter, as well."

Sam looked at him inquiringly. His gentle eyes were still concerned about the widow of the commander of the 54th Regiment.

"I think you would be the most appropriate person to go to South Carolina and express the sympathy of the Commonwealth to the entire 54th Regiment. Would you be willing to do that?"

Startled, Sam stuttered, "Why, Governor Andrew! I am honored!" He was thinking quickly. He had not ever thought of having an opportunity to play such a large role in the war effort. What would this mean? How long would he be gone? How would his family fare? What would his role be?

"Can you give me some time to discuss this with my wife?" he answered, finally.

Governor Andrew said, "I am here for a week, in Lenox. I am reachable through the Shaw family."

Sam thanked him and took his leave. Walking towards

home he knew within a few minutes that he would accept this honor and go to South Carolina to give solace and comfort to those of the 54th Massachusetts Voluntary Infantry still stationed there. His excitement grew as he thought more and more about his mission. It would be a huge undertaking, a long journey, one fraught with great sadness, but also full of potential. He could be of help to these men and that felt right.

When he reached home and told Ellen she was at first taken aback. How long would he be gone? How would she manage without him? Sitting together at the kitchen table they mapped out the next few months, both feeling tremendous gratitude for their daughter Hester Jane, now nineteen years old, especially as their youngest daughter Lydia was just two years old. Hester had been helping with the household since they could remember. Without her his trip would be a hardship on the family. After determining that Ellen was satisfied that she could manage, Sam arranged to see Governor Andrew the next afternoon.

"Well Reverend Harrison," Governor Andrew said, "I am most pleased. I will see that the necessary papers are prepared." There was a moment's silence as the two of them considered the tasks each had in front of them now the decision was made.

"Ahem," said Governor Andrew, "another thing. Dr. Hopkins, ah, Mark Hopkins, you know him, yes?"

"Why yes, of course. The president of Williams College. We are well acquainted."

"Well, he has recommended you, a 'man of honor, good judgment and principles', says he, to become the Chaplain of the 54th. What say you? Your pay would be equal to that of the other commissioned officers."

"My, my!" replied Sam, "that is most gratifying! He did mention something to that effect earlier this month." Sam cleared his throat, emotions causing his voice to quaver. "Are there extra duties required of the chaplain other than to hold services and give comfort to the soldiers? Would I need extra training?"

Governor Andrew looked at him closely and shook his head. "You come highly recommended. A superior court judge told me you have been the means of great good here in Pittsfield and that your talents are of a high order. More need not be said! That is high praise indeed!" He smiled at Sam and thrust his hand towards him.

"Then it is arranged! Report for duty as soon as you can! Morris Island will be sweltering hot in August. The trip down will take a few days. Godspeed my good sir! And good luck!"

Sam shook the Governor's hand and they parted. The first leg of the journey from Boston to New York would be on a government ship. Arrangements for the rest of his trip from New York to South Carolina were up to him. That done, Sam left his home and family a few days later.

# Chapter 8

"Sir!" Sam saluted the officer in front of him. "Reverend Samuel Harrison reporting for service." He was in Beaufort, South Carolina and it was hot under the tent, despite its size. General Rufus Saxton, commander of the department in the South was flanked by two aides.

One aide eyed Sam without much interest. "Reporting for what kind of service, Sir?"

"Why, I am sent from Governor Andrew of Massachusetts, Sir," Sam replied.

"What kind of service, I said!"

"I am on a special mission to give comfort to the soldiers, Sir. Comfort to the men of the 54th Massachusetts Voluntary Infantry. May I ask where they are barracked?" Sam was feeling uncomfortably unwelcomed.

He was hot, tired and discouraged. His journey down had not been without complications and downright misery. On the second day of the journey, when he had reached New York the steamer on which he had made reservations was deemed "too full" to accommodate him and he was forced to wait for eight days for the next one, the *Arago*. Then he was told he could not receive his meals on the *Arago* because he was "a colored man." In protest he spoke to the captain, a Mr. Gadsden, telling him he was on his way to South Carolina to give solace to the soldiers fighting for the country. This held little weight with the captain who stubbornly refused to change his mind. And consequently he was forced to purchase the provisions for his own meals while still on land. Then, to add insult to injury, once on board, he was provided no place to sleep, was not allowed in the cabin to eat his meals, even during a storm, the reason being he was a "colored man." The next morning, having slept on the stairs all night an aggrieved and insulted Sam went to the back of the ship to write in his journal. The morning sun shone on his face and his damp clothes began to steam in the heat. He felt a little better but resolved to take his complaints to Captain Gadsden once again. He was putting his journal in his coat pocket when he heard a familiar voice:

"Reverend Harrison? Samuel Harrison? Is that you?" Sam turned around, the sun in his eyes, but still he recognized Colonel Higginson. The Reverend Thomas Wentworth Higginson was a colleague of Sam's. A passionate orator, he was an ardent abolitionist who had been one of the six secret men, along with Gerrit Smith, to fund John Brown's activities to fight against slavery in the 1850s.

"Why Colonel Higginson, Rev. Thomas! I was just wishing you to be on board, but thinking you in the South already!"

Colonel Higginson had also been recruited by Governor Andrew in November of 1862 to raise a Colored Regiment in the South: the First South Carolina Volunteers, the first Black regiment raised to fight in the war. It was composed of slaves freed in the South by the Union army.

95

"No, no! I am returning. My regiment is awaiting my arrival! What brings you here Rev. Harrison?"

Sam narrated his conversation with Governor Andrew just a few days before, mentioning also the poor treatment he had received at the hands of Captain Gadsden.

"Let me see to that, Rev. Harrison! That is no way to be treated! Then can we have breakfast together?"

Colonel Higginson went in search of the Captain. Sam tried to imagine what passed between them, racism and prejudice being completely foreign to Col. Higginson's heart. The issue was resolved and the rest of the trip passed without incident. Col. Higginson had been with the First South Carolina Volunteers since the previous November. His men were already experienced soldiers situated at Camp Saxton near Beaufort.

§§§

The aide looked at Sam. "Barracked? What regiment may I ask?"

"The regiment formerly under the command of Col. Robert Shaw, Sir!"

General Rufus Saxton, who had been writing a letter looked up at Sam.

"Ah yes," he said "you are Reverend Harrison?"

"I am, Sir, reporting for duty. Here are my papers."

"Ah, we are glad you have arrived! We've been expecting you! Your journey went well?"

Sam described his treatment under Captain Gadsden and how Col. Higginson had stepped in to speak up for him. The General assured him on his return journey he would be treated with respect.

"And you met Colonel Higginson aboard ship? Did you know him beforehand?"

"Why yes. We have been acquainted for some years. He is from Massachusetts, you know?"

"That I do know. I petitioned Governor Andrew to appoint him to take on the command of the First South Carolina Volunteers. I am glad you know him. He is a godly man and a true fighter for justice and equality, and a poet as well."

"And a pastor. A Unitarian minister." Sam smiled.

"Yes, quite," replied General Saxton. "For now, you will be at "Praise House" for the services. I suggest you find lodging in town. The barracks are not far from here. You," he said pointing to the aide, "Please escort Reverend Harrison to the barracks and then to town."

The aide looked at Sam and then back at General Saxton as if reluctant to walk in company with a Black man. Sam could feel the tension and knew he was again facing racial prejudice. "What are we fighting this war for?" he thought to himself with some bitterness.

"Go on then," said General Saxton to the aide, with a frown.

The aide sighed and turned on his heel, reluctantly leading the way. Despite the awkwardness, Sam was relieved to finally know where he was going and to find a place to lay his head. He was eager to meet the men and see who was still present of those who enlisted from back home.

Sam followed the aide first to the barracks. It was mid-day and the camp looked deserted. He wondered where everyone was. He thought about Eli Franklin and wondered how he had fared with his wounds. Taking courage to address the man who obviously did not want to be helping him, he asked whether he knew what had become of Eli. The aide answered curtly, "He succumbed to his wounds on the 31st of July, if I recollect rightly."

Sam sighed deeply. His task of bringing comfort to the soldiers from Berkshire would be a hard one. He thought of Eli's s wife Cornelia, sitting in their home in Pittsfield, waiting for news of her husband. And now he would have to write them of his death. "Oh my heart," he thought, "how will they be able to bear this?"

*Army Camp in Beaufort*

*Fort Wagner, Morris Island, Charleston Harbor, South Carolina*
*Barracks for the soldiers of the 54th Massachusetts*
*Volunteer Infantry*

The hot August sun beat down on his head as he looked around. He would come back in the evening. He nodded to the aide that he had seen enough and asked the way to town. He had decided to spend the rest of the day becoming acquainted with Beaufort. He knew it had once been the resort of wealthy and cultured white people and he was curious to see some of its charm. And also perhaps visit an old friend of his, a Dr. William Henry Brisbane, former pastor at Pipe Creek Baptist Church in Beaufort.

Years ago, after Sam had returned from his school in Ohio and was back working on the shoe bench, he had become acquainted with Dr. Brisbane, a former slaveholder in Beaufort. At the time of their meeting in Philadelphia Dr. Brisbane had recently emancipated the slaves he had inherited from his father. To do this he had to move to Cincinnati, Ohio because South Carolina state law forbade the emancipation of ones' slaves. He had moved his whole family and plantation of slaves to Ohio and then provided the enslaved people their emancipation papers. His previous income had come from the work the slaves had done in the cotton and indigo fields. And consequently he had become quite without any earnings, and his family was destitute. His friends, hearing of his plight, got together some funds to send him to Philadelphia. Once there, he founded a newspaper in the interest of human freedom. Sam, needing extra money himself for his further schooling, had sold over 200 subscriptions to this paper and thus had become acquainted with Dr. Brisbane. They had a deep respect for one another and Sam now went in search of him. He had heard that Dr. Brisbane was back in Beaufort, in his old residence, working in a government office dedicated, ironically, to the war effort. He was directed to a lovely colonnaded home on the main street. He looked admiringly at the tropical foliage: bougainvillea, hibiscus, oleander. "Even during a war we have such beauty," he thought paradoxically. Then he knocked on the door, which was opened by a tall, stately Black woman.

Tipping his hat he said: "I am newly arrived in Beaufort and looking to have an audience with Dr. Brisbane. Would you be so kind as to inform him it is Reverend Samuel Harrison."

Henrietta, who was a freed slave now in Dr. Brisbane's employ, nodded, ushered him into the parlor and went in search of Dr. Brisbane.

"My God, fellow! Good to see you, Sir! And here in Beaufort! Who would have thought it?" Dr. Brisbane clapped his hands on Sam's back, enveloping him in a warm embrace. "I had heard from General Saxton that you might be coming down! But I had no idea it would be this soon! Why Rev.

Samuel Harrison! How good you look! It's wonderful to see you!"

Sam was overwhelmed. Here he had thought he was traveling to enemy country, foreign and wild and already he had met two good friends. They sat and talked as Henrietta served a sumptuous tea with cucumber sandwiches, seed cakes and a peach tart. "You still get good food here, even during a war!" Sam said as the peach tart slipped sweetly down his throat. He said it partially in jest, but also as a true observation.

"Why, yes," Dr. Brisbane said sheepishly, "My situation has improved since you last saw me! I now have a steady income and much help around the home and garden."

Sam had been looking around the room. "You lived here before you emancipated your slaves?"

"Yes, yes, this house has been in the family for generations."

"You gave up a lot when you emancipated the people working for your family. I am gratified and impressed. One never knows quite what southern gentlemen have to wrestle with when considering the emancipation question. I can see this would be a difficult decision, to part with a place such as this."

"We had two houses. This is our town house. The other, the one I gave up, is a plantation south of here in the low country on the Stono River Estuary. That is where most of our slaves were and where our income came from. I am glad it is gone. It is a place cursed with misery and suffering."

"But still," countered Sam, "it was certainly a grave decision and I respect you the more for it. Our danger, the danger for this country, is that men of no character and great ambition have ample opportunity to rise to the highest positions in the land. Then we are truly on the path to complete ruin. But with you as a model, the future might be brighter."

Dr. Brisbane nodded wryly. "In the end it was not a difficult decision for me. It was like a dream I'd had since I was a young boy. I grew up playing with Nat, the son of our cook. At first I saw no difference between us; we were the same age, and the same build and abilities. We played every day. Our friendship was deep and real. But then, when I began my schooling, he was not allowed to join me. This caused me great distress and confusion. Our lives went down different paths thereafter. I was not able to determine my own path, nor he his. I had the best education had to offer, while he had nothing but toil and labor. I felt this separation sorely. While studying to become a minister I tried to make sense of what was all around me. I even tried to promote slavery. I preached it as the natural order of things. But when my father died and I inherited the place I was no longer able to turn a blind eye to the ignominy, to the dishonor to these people I had known my whole life. I began to preach abolition. This brought shame to my family and congregation and I was barred from my church. I became the "worst enemy of the South, a traitor to the cause!" I betrayed my heritage and became a hated man in Beaufort and beyond. However, I was determined to do what was right. My allegiance could not be to my father's memory, it had to be to my conscience." Dr. Brisbane mopped his forehead and admitted, "It did take a lot of planning and a long time for my dream to come to fruition. But in the end, it was not a hard decision, no it was not. I have no regrets." Dr. Brisbane sighed and then smiled wryly. "Incidentally, I have been appointed by the U.S. government as chairman of the U.S. Direct Tax Commission for South Carolina and I am responsible for confiscating the plantations of the very people who hated me so."

Sam sat silent for a while. His heart felt deeply moved. This man had done a great deed even if he did not admit it. He decided to introduce him to Col. Higginson. He felt it would increase the understanding between North and South, even if only among like-minded people.

Sam thought of the Bolton family, the family that had owned his parents and freed them when he was three years old. He pondered what a process of judgment that had been, although he knew it was based more on economic necessity. He mentioned this to Dr. Brisbane who agreed that it was a complicated path, but reiterated that it was not hard to take if one abhorred the institution of slavery.

They parted and Sam went back to the barracks to see the brave men of the 54th. He sought out Charles Potter, his neighbor on Third Street in Pittsfield to get the news of the general health and mood of the 54th. Sam had been instrumental in getting Charles to enlist and he felt a special fondness for the boy, only eighteen years old. He found Charles sitting with his friend Isaiah Welch who had been with him on the assault on Fort Wagner. Charles was in a positive mood and gave Sam a glowing report about their activities since arriving in South Carolina. Sam said he was particularly interested to hear about the battle on Morris Island to secure Fort Wagner.

"We stood upon the parapets surrounding our giant cannon, the 'Swamp Angel' and saw men fall around us like hailstones," said Isaiah Welch. "We stood fast and kept the men who were working upon them together as much as possible. The enemy fired shell and grape into us like hot cakes, but we kept at our work like men of God."

"We heard only the beat of drummer boy instructing us to advance or halt or retreat or ceasefire. That and the sight of the flag kept us upright and charging," said Charles.

Sam looked at the two of them admiringly. "Truly I have the deepest respect for you!" he exclaimed. "You have done so well, shown such courage and discipline."

"It is truly amazing," continued Isaiah. "We, who in the past could scarcely walk down a street in our home cities without fearing for our lives even in the most suppliant of conditions, now march in solid platoons, with shouldered muskets, slung knapsacks and buckled cartridge-boxes down our gayest avenues and busiest thoroughfares to the strains of martial music!"

"We are celebrated and saluted," agreed Charles. "What a prodigious revolution the public mind is experiencing!"

"That is certainly true," agreed Sam. "That is truly thrilling news to report back home. That is what we like to hear, that our efforts are successful, that we are recognized for who we always were. Well done, men."

"I can say ... that I do not regret the moment I enlisted in defense of my country, which is fighting for the defense of liberty and the rights of my enslaved brothers and sisters who are in bondage," said Isaiah.

Sam settled into the rhythm of life in the barracks, ministering daily to the soldiers, writing letters home for them, giving counsel to help them be strong when faced with loss, suffering and pain. He also held services for all the troops, no matter whether they were Baptist, Presbyterian, Unitarian, Methodist or Congregational, four times on Sunday and twice during the week, as well as evening praise meetings.

He regularly visited the wounded soldiers in the hospital in Beaufort. Eighteen had been wounded on James Island and 149 on the assault on Fort Wagner. He brought them encouraging words and some news of home. Three he knew from the Berkshires: Sam Weaver had been wounded in the arm, and Valorous Williams in the chest and Peter Pruyn in the eye. He spent extra time with them whenever he could.

"How are things at home, Reverend Harrison?" asked Peter Pruyn.

"To tell the truth it was very hot and humid there also when I left, that I can well say," replied Sam.

He was sitting with Valorous and Peter outside in the shade by the hospital terrace. He was worried that Peter would never see again. Both eyes were bandaged.

"But not as hot as here, I wager," chimed in Valorous.

Sam smiled. "No, I suppose not. But the plums were getting ripe and the peaches in the orchard on North Street were plump and ready to pick."

"Did you bring us any?" quipped Peter, trying to keep his mind off of his wounds. "We don't get many here." The tears kept leaking into his bandages. Not being able to see was frightening.

"Tell us, Reverend Harrison," interrupted Valorous in an attempt to ward off too much emotion, "what news of home do you have?"

Sam began telling them of Pittsfield and their families. He had come armed with letters from each of their parents. Peter's letter contained news of his sister's newborn son, Jedidiah, as well as a photograph of the bride and groom on their wedding day. Sam strove to do the photograph justice by describing every detail of their clothing and demeanors. He tried to avoid looking at Peter's face as he talked, putting his hand on Peter's arm to give comfort for his loss.

He began to steer the conversation to a recounting of the battle to claim Fort Wagner. He knew they were proud of themselves and the regiment. The attack had been spearheaded by the 54th.

"We were fighting under Sergeant Major Lewis Douglass. He was a fine soldier who inspired our every step. He was wounded towards the end of the first assault. We became momentarily confused. It was a major blow. Then we heard Colonel Shaw shouting out: "Onwards Boys, Onwards" and that gave us the courage to keep on charging," said Valorous.

"I think the last thing I saw was our flag being held in place on the top of the ramparts," said Peter. He was silent for a while. Sam did not speak, allowing Peter to gather his thoughts. Sitting still and allowing the silence to grow, Sam felt the fear and frustration that had built up in Peter. He knew that he could do little other than listen, to help ease the pain.

As Sam was preparing to take leave of the men, Peter lifted his head and said, "I guess it was a good thing to know we were still upright and fighting though I myself had fallen. But that flag, it was a good last thing to see." He turned away and put his head in his arms. Valorous smiled up at Sam "I will see that Peter gets back to the ward, Reverend Harrison. Thank you for your visit."

They said goodbye and Sam returned to the barracks to get ready for the church service that afternoon.

Sam undertook his mission of comfort with a deepening respect and reverence for these men. They were willing to give their lives for this country. Whether that gift had been given perhaps now with regret was not relevant. Some of them had paid the ultimate price. He wished fervently he could make it better.

~

Thus his days were full. He met many former slaves, now freed people, who had been left behind when the Confederate army fled to the mainland. They had joined the Union army camps as laborers, cooks, laundry help and all-around camp aides. The majority of White plantation owners had fled their homes as the Union army marched through the South. Their slaves, naturally, took this opportunity to stay behind, freed by the Union army. Some had been "house-servants" and some had been "fieldhands", working on the cotton, rice and indigo plantations. He spoke with these people and learned a tremendous amount about this "institution of slavery" that he had not known before. Very few could read, few had skills beyond what they had been taught while working the plantations. They knew hard work. They had no trouble keeping up with the tasks assigned them. They took jobs in the camps, digging ditches, cleaning latrines, collecting food from the abandoned farms for the soldiers and themselves to eat. They cooked, they sewed, washed laundry, they marched with the regiments when moving camps. Their first taste of freedom was heady and thrilling. But the fact of their subjugation for so many years made Sam's heart heavy with the guilt of indifference and unawareness that had been shown these men, their families and their ancestors. This war, with all its bloodshed, devastation, death and suffering was being fought for a just and noble cause: to right the terrible wrongs and unbearable sorrows done to an entire race of people. He shuddered to think what was still in front of them as well as all that lay in the past.

*"In a prison cell I sit, thinking mother dear of you and our bright and happy home so far away ... Tramp, tramp, tramp the boys are marching! Cheer up comrades they will come. And beneath the starry flag, we shall breathe the air again, of the free land in our own beloved homes..."* Sam heard the singing coming from the camp. The men were singing the prison song to keep up their spirits. The soldiers who had been captured in the assault on Fort Wagner were in a prison camp not too far from them. Sam could only imagine their despair, how cut-off they felt from their comrades, their family and their country. He had heard that a group of soldiers from the 54th had paraded up and down close to the prison camp singing the song *"In a prison cell I sit, thinking mother dear of you, and our bright and happy home so far away ... So within the prison cell, we are waiting for the day, that you'll come to open wide the iron door ..."*

§§§

After five weeks, Sam felt his special mission of comfort had been accomplished and he was ready to return home. Before he left he was invited to accompany General Gilmore on a tour of Morris Island on which the battle of Fort Wagner had been so bravely fought. He stood at the bottom of a gently sloping dune looking up at the ramparts, which were visible just beyond the crest. Patches of sawgrass and stunted cypress cut into the horizon. As the sun broke through the clouds the fort was first in shadow and then so brightly lit as to be blinding. He shaded his eyes and tried to imagine the soldiers of the 54th charging towards those cannons without any thought in their minds other than they were going to capture the fort for the Union.

"You heard the story of Sergeant William Carney?"

General Gilmore asked Sam.

"Well, a part of it. I have heard from one of the wounded soldiers I've been tending that the flag held upright was the last thing he himself saw before he fell," answered Sam.

"It was an act of bravery of the highest order," said General Gilmore. "From what I heard, Carney was on high ground, close to the fort. He saw the soldier who was carrying the Union flag get shot in the back. Carney sprinted over, his eyes riveted on the flag, to catch the flag before it fell to the ground. Although himself wounded, he kept it aloft as the battle raged around him. Many men of the 54th were fighting hand-to-hand combat within the fort by that time. But unfortunately they were driven back by the Confederate soldiers at the close of the day." He paused, taking a deep breath.

*Sergeant William Harvey Carney*

Sam was silent. He could almost hear the sound of battle still echoing from the ramparts. He started when General Gilmore continued his story. "They were well trained, the men under Col. Shaw. We were astounded and then deeply gratified, at their discipline and valor under extremely difficult circumstances, even as we went about our own business."

Again he was silent, shading his eyes with his hand as the sun emerged from the clouds. Then he continued:

"The regiment was made the 'storming party.' They were the men in the forefront of the battle. The Union troops were trying to secure the fort that afternoon. The fighting was fierce ... I was there, I saw it all from the beachhead where my men were manning the 'Swamp Angel' our mighty cannon. In the end it mattered not that they lost that particular battle. The entire nation saw that each soldier had performed with "bravery and discipline."

Sam nodded. He had heard this from the men themselves as well as their commanding officers. In the meantime the entire island was now secured for the Union troops. And each soldier expressed a "readiness to meet the enemy again." Many of the men had also mentioned their grief at the loss of their Colonel Robert Gould Shaw, as well as the wounding of Sergeant Major Lewis Douglass, the son of Frederick Douglass. Sergeant Major Douglass had been elevated to the highest ranking Black officer of the 54th and had participated in the storming of Fort Wagner. He later wrote to his fiancée, Amelia Loguen: *"The regiment has established its reputation as a fighting regiment, not a man flinched, though it was a trying time. Men fell all around me. A shell would explode and clear a space of twenty feet. Our men would close up again, but it was no use, we had to retreat, which was a very hazardous undertaking. How I got out of there alive I cannot tell, but I am here."*

~

General Gilmore assured Sam that the battle was a pivotal one and proved once and for all that Black troops would fight with discipline and bravery if only given the chance.

Sam returned to Boston on a government ship, the same one he had come down on, the *Arago*. This time he had a place to sleep and was served his meals with the others. The color of his skin was not remarked upon. Despite the suffering he had witnessed in the South he felt already some small progress in the relations between the races had already occurred. "This is what hope looks like," he thought to himself.

*The Assault on Fort Wagner*

# Chapter 9

"You make me so proud dear Sam." Ellen was near to tears. "I cannot imagine what it was like for you seeing so much suffering. Come Hester. Let us bring out the plum jam to have with this cake."

Hester Jane was bustling around her father. His return had lightened her load of cares appreciably but she saw how distracted he was when he wasn't engaged in direct conversation with them.

"Oh Papa! You saw Charles Potter?" Hester inquired, trying to bring her father's thoughts back to the present. "How was he doing? Was he wounded?"

Sam smiled at her. "No dear, he was not wounded. He fought bravely under Sergeant Major Lewis Douglass." Sam was aware of his distraction and determined to focus again on his family. They were sitting in the front room, a cozy fire in the grate, all faces turned eagerly towards him.

"Yes, children. They fought bravely and have surely earned the reputation as a fighting-regiment. They never flinched, shells exploding everywhere. They have done us proud. And they have established our reputation as brave, fearless and disciplined soldiers. I am proud to be associated with them."

Ellen smiled. She knew what a toll this had taken on her husband. "Children, Papa has something more to tell us, don't you Sam?"

Sam hesitated and then nodded. "While I was in Boston and visiting Governor Andrew to receive my pay I heard that I have been given my army commission to be the Chaplain of the 54th Regiment."

The children sat silent and big-eyed.

"This means that I will again be traveling to the South." He paused, looking at them. "This is a great honor for your father. It will be hard on you, I know. But you have each other." He paused again. "I do not yet know when I will be going but I will receive my orders within the month...."

No one knew whether to be happy or sad. They understood the honor of this post, and also that it meant he would have to be away for some time.

Ellen passed around small pieces of oat cake topped with plum jam. Hester poured out hot tea with milk and honey. It made a festive mood and they all forgot for a little while that their father would be leaving them again so soon.

"Tell us more stories, Papa," said one of his children. "Tell us what it is like in the South."

"Well, I did meet some remarkable people," replied Sam. "There is a woman; her name is Susie King Taylor. She was fourteen years old when the Union troops came through. She was freed and brought with hundreds of other freed people to Simon's Island off the coast of South Carolina, near where I was staying. She had been taught to read and write as a child and therefore, at that young age, she was made a teacher to all the children. When I arrived in Beaufort she was at Camp Saxton, a former plantation that is now an army camp under the command of Colonel Higginson. She was not only a teacher but a nurse and cook, whatever task she took up she was good at. Everyone loved her. I met her at the hospital in Beaufort working with the nurse Clara Barton who was in charge of our wounded men of the 54th." Sam paused musingly. "I saw that they all were in good hands with these two women! That is a comfort because some of the men were truly in need of special care." Sam looked wistfully at his children's faces knowing he wouldn't see them for a while. He gave a quick prayer to God for their protection.

~

That evening Sam mentioned to Ellen, "it is an interesting fact of war that Susie King Taylor told me. She said that when she first joined Colonel Higginson's regiment she was almost struck immobile by the severity of the wounds these soldiers received, hands blown off, legs decimated, gaping head wounds. But after a while she was able to just evaluate the injuries as they came in and do what was needed to help. She said this was her real growing up."

Ellen remarked that war was good for no one while it was going on.

"You are so right," replied Sam. "But it's a war we have to fight. While in the South Colonel Higginson made me aware of a pamphlet written by Moses Roper, an escaped slave. His narrative is so harrowing I could barely read it. The suffering, the degradation, the torture and cruelty he experienced in the first seventeen years of his life, before his escape, makes me despair for humanity. How can there be such cruelty? He escaped sixteen or seventeen times before he finally made his way to England and was freed. On his many escapes and returns to his cruel master, he became aware of God and Christianity and divine grace. He cared so much about his own soul that, when he reached England, he was baptized in a church to save his soul. Eventually he was able to be educated at a school and university, aided by abolitionists who took him in. He said, when he wrote his narrative, that upon looking back upon his life, he regretted the *deception* it took for him to gain his freedom. My goodness. How blighted this world is." Sam sighed. "This is why we have to fight. This is why people have to die. This is why I have to return to the South. There is so much need. It is for a just cause. And yet I can barely uphold the sentiment that the ends justify the means. There is such cruelty it defies the imagination." He put his head down on his arms. He mumbled through his sleeve. "As it is said, 'all that is needed for evil to triumph is for good men to do nothing'..... I cannot do nothing."

Ellen took her husband in her arms and held him until he was calm enough to go to bed.

~

Despite having been being paid for the six weeks Sam had been in the South, money was tight. He knew it was a hardship for his family to be left alone with no visible means of support. Together he and Ellen inspected the larder for stores that she had laid by for the winter. The squash, pumpkins, onions and potatoes looked to be sufficient but the carrots had been scarce over the summer due to a meal-worm infestation. They purchased a barrel of flour to augment their store. The apples were kept under the staircase in two barrels layered with straw. Their flock of chickens was still thriving, though the eggs were coming fewer and fewer as the days grew shorter and the winter darkness set in. The pig had been butchered, salted and hung in the chimney to be smoked. Sam had to borrow funds to obtain his uniform and supplies, as well as travel money. He gave whatever was left to Ellen to keep the family through the time he was away. He knew he would be paid at least the army wage of $13 per month and perhaps more as a chaplain which he had heard would be $100 per month. If this were indeed so, then he could begin sending money home in December and that would help keep his family from hunger.

In the beginning of November Sam received his marching orders. He traveled to Boston and met with the adjutant of the Commonwealth who ordered him to report to Morris Island as soon as possible. As fate would have it, he was again aboard the *Arago*. This time it was different. He was a commissioned officer, a full-fledged army chaplain, recognized by the officers on board. He had no trouble with the Captain and was accorded mostly the same respect as the White officers.

# Chapter 10

"I am authorized to assure you that you will receive the same wages, the same rations, the same equipment, the same protection, the same treatment and the same bounty, secured to the white soldiers...." Sam was recalling the words spoken by Frederick Douglass to a group of men in April of the year before when such great effort was being made to raise colored troops in the North to fight in the war. He had gathered them in the hall of the church telling them that the war being waged to end the institution of slavery logically should include colored men fighting for their right to be free and equal. They knew the stakes were high. They had heard that if one of them were captured by the southern army they would be immediately enslaved, or executed. It did not still their fear to know that President Lincoln had decreed that, "for every captured Black Union soldier the Confederacy enslaves, a rebel soldier will be placed at hard labor in retaliation." Still the response was mostly positive. The dignity of receiving equal pay, equal food, the same tents and equipment, was very appealing. Many of the young men had families to support or elderly parents for whom they were responsible. The guarantee of an income pretty much clinched the deal. Although all of them were free, they knew hundreds of thousands of their race were not. As a result they enlisted in regiment after regiment and were deployed to the South. The dream of the pay they would receive comforted many as they suffered the rigors of preparing for battle.

Sam shook his head. What a delusion that had been! He had been mustered for a month and was looking forward to his first payday. In conversation with Colonel Hallowell, second in command to their colonel and a kindly gentleman, Sam had been informed that he probably would not receive the same wages as the white chaplains. In some confusion Sam asked where he had heard this. "From the paymaster, just this morning," was the reply.

"Well, I would like to see him myself, then!" responded Sam. Sam made his way to the paymaster's tent, but the paymaster had come and gone. The white officers had gotten their pay but the rank and file had been neglected. Not even informed. Sam thought of Ellen and his family preparing for the Christmas season, looking to have a little extra for treats and presents. It was discouraging enough that the Black soldiers had to fight under White officers without the possibility of obtaining the rank of an officer, but not to receive pay when promised it! While fighting for equality they were not to be treated as equal? The irony was blinding. The White soldiers were receiving $13 per month with an occasional $3 extra given in the form of clothing. Many of the Black soldiers had been told that they would receive $10 per month with the occasional $3 *deducted* from that for clothing. When the soldiers had been offered their first pay that past June, every one of them had refused to take the lower amount.

"We did not come to fight for money, for if we did we might just as well have accepted the money that was offered us; we came not only to make men of ourselves, but also our colored brothers at home," said Isaiah Welch when he was informed of this discrepancy.

They were fulfilling their obligations as soldiers but not being paid. At that point, before their first real taste of war and the assault on Fort Wagner, their commander, Colonel Shaw, had written a letter to Governor Andrew proclaiming that his men would not accept a lower pay. Informed of the matter, Governor Andrew concurred that this was the right move and began petitioning the War Office for a decision, claiming it was not lawful to withhold pay for soldiers correctly mustered. However, it was countered that The Militia Act of July 1862 had stipulated that persons of African descent were to be hired as *manual laborers* helping the war effort by building fortifications and digging trenches and were hence to be paid at a lower rate. To the paymaster it did not seem to matter that the men of the 54th and 55th Regiment were soldiers fulfilling their duties. He was going by the color of their skin, not their status or their signed contract with the government.

"That Militia Act was surely meant for those freed slaves who joined the Union Army as it came through their area," Sam said to Dr. Brisbane on his weekly visit to his home. "They have been hired to do manual labor, skilled or unskilled. How can they interpret it as meaning *anyone* of African descent?"

"It certainly puts a damper on one's spirit to think of such gross misinterpretation of the Act," replied Dr. Brisbane sympathetically. "I remember hearing that early in the war, I think it was within the first weeks, that three slaves escaped their masters and under cover of darkness rowed across the harbor to claim asylum at the Union's Fort Monroe. This was in Virginia, at Jamestown, I think. Major General Butler, who was but a short time at his post, declared them contraband. He was originally a lawyer and knew the law, the Fugitive Slave Law that mandated slaves be returned. But then, he rationalized, it was a war and Virginia had seceded from the Union. Virginia could be considered a sovereign nation and consequently Butler alleged the Fugitive Slave Law did not apply. He was not obliged to return the men and, he further reasoned, that since the slaves had been building fortifications to destroy the Union fort ... they could be seen as weapons of war! And so, as contraband, he did not return them and they were the first slaves freed by the war, ironically not far from the settlement where slavery started in 1619. I think the Militia Act was created to deal with just that kind of situation. Not for soldiers properly mustered in the army." Dr. Brisbane sighed. "Soldiers mustered under Col. Higginson can be confusing the issue, I think," Dr. Brisbane continued. "His regiment consists of freed slaves who were found competent to serve, trusted to be trained and armed to fight. I think the Militia Act is being willfully misinterpreted to mean even those soldiers who had always been free and had mustered in the North."

Sam was silent. He had not heard these stories and it made him think. "I will do my best to make this right. Our soldiers are doing their duty, fulfilling their contract, the government must make good on their promise. I will see what I can do."

Before the assault on Fort Wagner, Governor Andrew and the Massachusetts legislature offered to pay the difference in the soldiers' pay out of the State's coffers. But the men refused. They knew that this was a matter of principle and all the Black soldiers in all the regiments were entitled to equal pay from the federal government. If they accepted Gov. Andrew's generous offer it would weaken their case for the rest of the colored troops from other states.

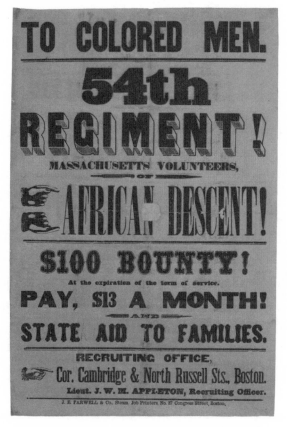

*Broadside used to recruit the men of the 54th promising equal pay and a $100 Bounty upon completion of service*

# Chapter 11

Ellen had written a cheery letter on Christmas Eve. They sounded as though they were doing fine but Sam could read between the lines. "We have all made little gifts for one another. Hester has knitted mittens for us all and little Ellen and Mary have strung the sweetest garlands of pine boughs that fill the house with such a delicious scent we all feel festive. We are planning quite the inventive Christmas meal and will surely have what we need to make a Christmas pudding ..."

They were scraping the bottom of the barrel, so to speak, he could tell. His heart ached to think of them bravely making do while he could do nothing to make their days easier. "Why must my family suffer so much just because I am Black, because I hail originally from an African nation? Where is the justice in that?"

He sat down to write an encouraging letter back. He would also put on a brave face.

Sam was preparing himself for his second visit to the paymaster, Officer Ten Eyck's tent. Already in January the air was heavy and warm. There had been a storm at sea and grey clouds hung on the horizon. He could hear the waves washing on the shore. Seagulls screamed as they fought over a dead sea-bass lying exposed on the beach. As he made his way towards the tent, Sam felt sick to his stomach. Would this indignity be repeated this time again? He felt his inner resources were growing thin.

What was a chaplain in the army to receive? He had been told $100 per month plus two rations a day ... and now nothing? He made his way towards the paymaster's tent. It was the end of January, 1864.

"Sir, I have come for my pay."

Officer Ten Eyck looked at Sam, his eyes traveling from his face down his uniform, pausing at his shoulders which showed his rank, and on down his legs to his feet, clad in brown leather boots. Then he looked down at his desk, took off his spectacles and placing his quill in the inkwell he said pointedly, "I have nothing for you."

"I am an officer in the Union army. I have carried out my obligation to my men. Should I not be paid?"

"I am only following orders. You and your men are to be paid the same as laborers, or not at all."

"And why is that?'

"You are of African descent" he said coldly.

Sam was stung. Such an openly racist and derogatory comment had not been uttered in his presence since he had set foot in the camp. He looked the officer in the eye. The man's face was hard and Sam knew it was of no use to pursue the issue at this time. He turned on his heel and left the tent, his anger growing to a low boil.

Sam began to be obsessed by the callous assault on his humanity and the humanity of his race. Wasn't this war being fought for social justice as well as racial justice? Hadn't the

Black soldiers proved themselves beyond doubt to be capable, brave and disciplined? Hadn't they enlisted in part because they had been promised equal pay and equal treatment and benefits? Was their presence as a fighting force not considered worth as much as a white soldiers? Sam's stomach tensed. He was supposed to give comfort to his men, and this he could do through thoughts of God and words from the Bible, but when asked about the inequities perpetrated by fellow human beings his ability to comfort failed him. He began to have trouble sleeping. His stomach began to bother him more and more. He felt impotent and ineffective. What was he to do? Where should he turn?

Christmas had come and gone. His letters to his family echoed the anguish he was feeling and the responsibility he carried for the welfare of his men. Ellen's letters put a brave face on their situation but Sam knew the truth. Their stores of food were growing thin. He knew the children were probably cold, as well. The thought from the Bible "I will not leave thee nor forsake thee" helped to sustain Sam as he carried out his mission of comfort. Occasionally he wondered how a merciful God could sanction such suffering and savagery, but quickly put the thought from him as unworthy of his faith.

"I am a man of God, am I not? I am a man of faith and this faith will keep me strong," he repeated to himself. "And this strength will give me the courage to right this wrong, to fight for my people." His men did not deserve to hear his doubts. They were troubled enough as it was.

And thus began Sam's second war, the war to make real what had been promised. The men of the 54th and the 55th had agreed unanimously not to accept the lower pay and instead to wait until what had been promised them was forthcoming.

The rest of the Black troops followed this same tactic. Even though it meant their families would do without, the soldiers stood firm. And Sam was aware that one avenue of rectifying the situation lay with him. He was acquainted with a number of men in positions of power. He would begin with another letter to Governor Andrew, and he would encourage the men in the regiment also to write.

A week later he heard back from Governor Andrew:

~

*My dearest Reverend Harrison,*

*"I have written to President Lincoln on your behalf. I especially mentioned to him the fact that you are a commissioned officer fulfilling a sacred office, that of chaplain. In the ancient church of Rome the road to positions of high dignity and honor have always been open to men of African descent. Not just priesthood but even bishoprics have been filled by men of your complexion. Nor is color or national origin a reason to reject or receive in any Christian church a man of African descent. For the first time now in history has it happened that such a man is pronounced to be unworthy of secular recognition. I especially underlined the fact that 'A refusal by an Officer of the Executive Department to recognize the capacity and rights of this chaplain is alike in violation of the rights of the Christian church and the laws of Congress. This insult to Christianity itself must be rectified.' I await an answer. Until then I remain*

*Your obedient Servant*

*John A. Andrew*

~

Sam read the letter with a mixture of pride, and dismay. Pride that he was recognized as having the same rights as white chaplains but dismayed at the arrogance and deceit shown the cause.

"Where is our shame?" Sam fumed to himself. "This land of the free still has so much bigotry and racial discrimination even among the highest elected officials in Congress. To interpret a law meant for freed slaves working in the Union army camps as laborers, to mean all people of African descent officially mustered in the army was interpreting the facts to conveniently suit their bigotry."

He remembered one rationale for the lower wage for these freed men had been that besides their pay and daily rations, their mothers, wives and children would also gain their freedom. Why a law had to be enacted in the first place was depraved enough. But to interpret it then to include all people of African descent legally mustered into the army and performing their soldierly duties in defense of their country was shameful, demeaning and humiliating. These were two entirely different issues. The men were fulfilling their contracts and needed to be paid for this.

Sam's hope lay in the way Governor Andrew had outlined his argument as a violation of all Christianity. That spoke deeply to his heart. Men of the African race have reached the highest orders within the Christian churches. Only in this country, "the land of the free!" is the color of a man's skin a deciding factor in how he is viewed and treated. His pride was soothed by the words of the governor. It was good to know a man of his caliber and inclinations had reached such a high office. Not all was lost.

Sam mopped his face with his handkerchief. This war created waves of hope and of despair, like riding out a storm at sea. His men gave him pride and hope. The other men who had that much power over their lives, brought him to the brink of despair. Would nothing change?

He put the letter aside. Smoothing out his uniform jacket, straightening his shoulders and breathing deeply he set forth on his walk through the encampment to see what Officer Ten Eyck had for him this time. Suddenly he felt a rush of gratitude to Governor Andrew for taking up the fight with such firm conviction. It gave him confidence for a brief moment and courage to look the paymaster in the eye.

He entered the tent with a firm stride, bolstered by the knowledge that he was in the right.

"Sir, I am here again for my pay at the usual rate for commissioned officers." Sam stood as tall as he could, his face a mask of unconcern.

"And that rate is $10."

"That rate is $100 per month plus two rations per day."

"As I have informed you before, I am under the orders of the Militia Act of 1862. You are not eligible for the higher rate as an *employee* of the Union army and a man of *African descent.*"

Sam stood stubbornly refusing to shift his gaze from Officer Ten Eyck's face.

"I am an *officer* in the Union army. *Not* an employee."

"These are my orders. You either take the $10 or I will give you nothing," Officer Ten Eyck continued, not taking his eyes from Sam.

Sam continued to stand there. Suddenly he felt unable to move. His feet felt like lead. A part of him could not comprehend what he had heard. Officer Ten Eyck's eyes wavered. He looked down at his desk, unsure what to do. Finally he sat down. He kept his eyes down and on his desk.

Without looking up and refusing to recognize Sam's official title, he said "You are dismissed, Mr. Harrison."

Suddenly Sam felt crushed by this man's arrogance. He could hardly breathe. His legs turned of their own accord towards the opening and he stumbled from the tent. Outside he braced himself against a hitching post and stood there shuddering, stooping over to ease his stomach. He did not want to be seen in such a weakened state but his body refused to obey and stand up straight. Sam closed his eyes and willed his mind to take hold of his instincts. Three deep breaths. A long shuddering sigh. He straightened a little. Three more deep breaths. "Lord, give me strength, Lord give me peace." He breathed deeply, and let his breath out slowly. He was standing straight, dizzy but a little calmer. He opened his eyes. "I am here, at Hilton Head.... I am alive and well.... I have not been physically injured.... I am ready to return to my men.... God is with me. All will be well," he said to himself.

As he stood there, with the sound of the waves lapping against the shore, the rustling of the dune grasses and the winter breeze blowing across his face, he was acutely aware of all the colored men who had fought for their race and died on this coast; and of their bodies lying under the sands and in mass graves. Their lives mattered, their sacrifice must be made to mean something. The future mattered. He took another deep breath, taking a wisp of courage from the thought of the future and let it out slowly. He could go on, he would prevail with God's help. These were, after all, soldiers of God and their cause was just.

His first steps were heavy. His stomach was still clenching. Each step he took away from the paymaster's tent gave him a little more strength to go on. He dodged a horse and cart carrying provisions to the mess hall, tripping over the sandy edges of the passageway between the tents. The winter sun shone weakly on the passersby casting a hazy glow around their heads. He passed a group of soldiers standing around a small cook fire, waving chunks of meat at each other as they laughed and joked. As he trudged by a gust of wind pushed gray wood-smoke in his direction. He stopped and took a deep breath and his walk grew firmer; not as many people looked curiously at him as he made his way back. By the time he returned to the camp he was feeling more in control. He tried to pass unobserved into his tent so he could have some time to gather his thoughts and figure out what to tell his men. But as he walked down the neat rows of tents the men crowded around him.

"What happened?" called out Charles Potter as he hurried along behind Sam.

"How did it go?" cried Isaiah.

Sam gestured for the men to get him a camp stool. He sat down on it heavily. Everyone could already tell it had not gone well.

Edward Washington, from Philadelphia, said "Reverend Harrison, put us out of our misery. Tell us what you have heard!"

"Hey! Are we going to get paid what we were promised?" chorused two more.

Sam looked at all the men gathered around. They had been giving their lives for their race and their country since the past July. He shook his head. Maybe this was a White man's war! Not one Black soldier had been paid. How much longer could this go on?

A breeze blew up from the shore and Sam took a deep

breath and looked back at the soldiers.

"Men, we must remain strong ..." he paused... "No, we have not yet achieved our goal ... Yes, we must remain soldiers of a Christian God. I know we all have families who are becoming destitute. And I know we promised to send our wages home...."

He looked at the men in their uniforms, ready to fight for the cause and he resolved to give them courage. "I know we were told what appears to be a pack of lies before we enlisted. But we *must carry on*. This will be resolved in our favor. We are all men of faith. We never imagined we would be in a war like this, a war of abolition, that we would be fighting for the rights of *our* race to be free. And yet here we are, yes, giving our lives to fight for what we believe in. And yes, we are not being paid but *we will be*."

Each emphasis on the words gave Sam power to continue. "Governor Andrew is advocating for us. He has written to President Lincoln. Our time will come. For the present we must tighten our belts, write hopeful letters to our families, bow our heads in prayer and carry on." Sam wiped the sweat from his brow. He was gathering strength from his resolve to remain positive for his men.

"We are not paid because our skin is Black. We are put beneath the very lowest of the low. We have not brought disgrace by cowardice! We have nothing to be ashamed of," said Edward Washington.

"Why should there be a distinction made between soldiers of a different nationality? Black face, white face, black hair, yellow hair, we all have red blood in our veins, we all die the same death," said William Parret.

"If it had been White soldiers who didn't receive their pay

the whole land would have been in a blaze of indignation...."

"We are willing to suffer all privations incidental to a Christian and a soldier!" said Isaiah, "but why should our families have to suffer destitution, as well?"

"How do the authorities expect our families to live without the means to buy bread, pay house rent in these terrible times?" said Parret.

"Yeah! It's our families we are concerned about above all!" cried someone from the back of the crowd.

"My wife has been ill for three months. How do I tell her to keep strong if there is no money for food or medicine to help her get well?"

"My wife has asked for 50 cents to help with the groceries. Fifty cents, man! How can this disdainful government expect our families to live?"

"Patience is a virtue, but it will soon cease to be so with us."

"How can it be expected that a soldier will do his duty under these circumstances? We are fighting for freedom and equality. And we fight so no one can say the White soldier has freed us! We, we will have freed ourselves, the Black soldier will have freed our own people. We ask for nothing more. "

The crowd was yelling out all at once, their frustration finding articulation in the group. The words swirled around Sam's head. He felt dizzy with fatigue and distress. He must have called out because suddenly it was silent.

Then a strong quiet voice spoke clearly to everyone. "I pray God the time will soon come when we, as soldiers of God, and of our race and country, may again face the enemy with boldness. If I fall in battle, remember, I fall in defense of my race and country." It was Isaiah Welch. He had a look on his face that told the men perhaps enough had been said.

Sam looked up at him in appreciation. Here was someone who carried a badge of courage able to rally the morale of this blessed regiment. He got up from his stool.

"Men, men! That's well said! Let's focus on the matter at hand. We will prevail! We shall win this war and we shall be paid a soldier's wage! All shall be well, and all manner of things shall be well! We shall not forget the words of the Bible. God will provide. We do not need to fear that God will not visit the righteous, for He is a just God and His justice will not slumber forever. Men make mistakes. We will make them aware of their error! We will continue to petition the War Office and the President. In the meantime, let's take courage in our collective intention to hold out for what is rightfully ours."

He saluted his men. "And remember: 'What is possible for human strength will become possible through the power of God.' That is from Luke in the 18th Chapter. I will see you at prayer service in the morn."

Sam bade his men goodbye and made a quiet retreat to his tent. He was tired. He had always had a melancholy streak that occasionally threw a wet cloak over his fiery energy. He felt that happening now. He needed to rest. His stomach felt in knots.

# Chapter 12

That night the wind picked up and began to howl around the camp. The tents flapped and swayed perilously in the gusts. Rain whipped under the canvas. Sleep was impossible. Sam tossed and turned. He felt hot, his brow damp with sweat. How could he continue in this misery? He was barely eating and was sleeping poorly. He was worried about his family; he was worried about his men. It was February and he had heard rumors that they would be breaking camp and making an expedition to northern Florida, to help with the siege on Jacksonville. His heart felt sick. Another battle, another dance with death, no end in sight. "And what if the widows of these brave and selfless men don't get a real widow's pension?" This new thought sent him deeper into misery. He felt weak, unable to raise his head. He knew he would not have the strength to accompany the 54th on this new expedition. He pulled his blanket over his ears to block out the wind. And moaned.

The next morning the regiment was ordered to break camp. The clouds had been blown away and the sky was a bright blue. The soldiers seemed energized and ready for their new mission. Sam ventured out of his tent to get a sense for his own health and also the mood of his men. His head felt woozy. He made his way to the mess tent, meeting a lieutenant-colonel along the way. The officer drew up his horse and commented on Sam's appearances: "You look like a ghost Reverend Harrison! How do you feel?"

Sam looked up at him with a weak smile, "You can see my condition, can you not?"

"If I were in command I would excuse you from embarking with your regiment to Florida. I rather think the Colonel would agree with me." He saluted and went on his way.

At the mess tent Sam saw the colonel and declared he was not well enough to continue to the next assignment.

"I cannot release you!" replied the colonel. He looked Sam over, "You look well enough to me, Reverend Harrison! Buck up! It can't be that bad. Be sure you are ready at noon!"

Sam knew he would have to find a way to get some rest before he did anything. He was making his way back to his tent when he saw the camp surgeon, a new friend of his.

"Are you going with the Regiment?" the surgeon inquired.

"I was hoping not to. You are aware of my condition. I am not well enough to make the trip."

"Then I will excuse you," said the surgeon. "Meet me in my tent and I will write up the release certificate."

When the surgeon finished writing out the paperwork he asked Sam to put out his tongue, which he did. "Reverend Harrison, I think you need to go to the hospital." He put his hand to Sam's forehead, "And you have a raging fever! Good God, man, you need to be off your feet and into bed!"

Sam nodded at him. "I have friends in Beaufort who could care for me. I just need a way to get there."

"I will make arrangements for your transport," said the surgeon.

§§§

"And then I was told no passes for Beaufort would be given out," said Sam to his friend Dr. Brisbane with whom he was staying. "He said the small pox was raging here. But I did get my pass when I mentioned your name. Anyway I went to a different quartermaster to see if I could be paid finally, having not a cent to my name."

Henrietta had brought in a pot of tea and some lemon and honey. "You need this, Reverend Harrison! It'll soothe your throat!"

Sam took the porcelain cup gratefully and ventured a sip. "I'll take more honey if you have it," he said wanly.

"Why surely Reverend Harrison, you have a sweet tooth, I can tell! And this is our very own Tupelo honey, extra special sweet!" She smiled at him, very happy to be able to do something for this dear sweet man who took so much on himself. When she had returned to the kitchen to get together a light evening meal Sam continued.

"So, there I was again at the paymaster's tent, only this was not the Ten Eyck fellow, it was another one in Hilton Head. When I asked him for my pay, even he said he could not pay me. When I asked why he said the same: "I cannot pay you because you are of African descent. This, I am afraid, bars you from being paid a regular chaplain's stipulated sum."

"I do the same work." I replied. "Is it just the color of my skin that bars me from getting paid the same wage?" By then I was so tired of the whole rigmarole and could not keep my temper from flaring, even with the fever. It made no sense to him, either but he said his hands were tied. I asked him to put this in writing which he did willingly. Of course he was only an assistant. But when I went to the chief paymaster, at his suggestion, the chief agreed. Nothing could be done! And so, here I am by the grace of God."

Sam lay back on the pillows. He had finished his tea and Dr. Brisbane poured him more with a generous dollop of the good honey and another squeeze of lemon.

"And now you are here!" he said looking fondly at Sam. "And we will take excellent care of you! Please consider this your home. Henrietta and I are so pleased to have you."

Sam nodded, content to let the rest, tea and affection begin the work of healing him.

By the end of the week, after much reflection and prayer around the condition of his health, Sam decided to request a furlough. He realized the hardest part of his tenure on Morris Island was having no money to send to his family. The worry about them added such stress to his system that he knew the only remedy was to see them himself. And, not less important, to attend to the issue of equal pay. Governor Andrew, in Boston, would be of essential assistance, but Sam wanted to be able to play a major part. He knew that if *he* felt so bad that he had become sickened by it, then surely the men in the regiments who had been here that much longer must be suffering equally. The only remedy would be petitioning the War Office and President Lincoln repeatedly until the matter was settled in their favor. He knew that a number of his men had also written to the President, one letter stating simply: "Your Excellency, We have done a Soldiers Duty. Why can't we have a Soldiers pay?"

It took two weeks for the request for a furlough to come back. He was pleased it had been granted and made a reservation on a steamer going north. He worried that he had no money with which to travel. In conversation with a fellow chaplain he was told, after much haggling, that he could be "advanced sixty dollars" with the understanding that he must refund it from his own pocket if the government did not side in the Black soldiers' favor. Having no other recourse, Sam took the money under those conditions and prepared for his departure.

He felt restricted by the manner in which he had received the money but could do nothing about it. He traveled north on the steamer *Fulton*, the *Arago* having left the week before.

The steamer *Fulton*

"You must sit beside me," said Mrs. Bewick. "I am sure the Captain would agree, wouldn't you, Captain Stanworth?"

Captain Stanworth nodded his head in agreement. Sam sat down to the right of Mrs. Bewick and to the left of Mrs. Wentworth. They had been south as part of a committee to bring food and clothing to the freed people of the Sea Islands. This was their return trip and they were full of good humor.

"We will be returning again very soon," said Mrs. Bewick. "The need is great and we have confidence this time we can raise the funds for at least two teachers to come with us."

"They will remain, of course," added Mrs. Wentworth. "The children need schooling!"

The women looked expectantly at Sam. "That is what I was doing also before I came south as a chaplain," replied Sam. "My work was in western Massachusetts and we sent three shipments down before I came south myself. There remains so much that still needs to be done."

He was feeling well enough to eat his whole dinner. Two days on board the *Fulton* with the bracing sea air bringing warmth to his cheeks, and the company of the most pleasant ladies from Boston, was doing wonders for his spirits. He trusted he was not just experiencing a "crest of hope" soon to be followed by a "trough of despair," that this was truly Divine Providence changing the course of his destiny.

The next day, as he was sitting on deck gazing out at the horizon his eye was caught by movement just outside the wake made by the ship. He saw the brown-yellow shell of a sea turtle just below the surface of the water. He noted concentric hexagons dappling its back. Its sudden appearance and beauty took his breath away. He looked again and saw there were two of them, riding just below the waves, rising and sinking and rising again, keeping pace with the ship. "And here we are amidst the carnage of war, the picture of man's inhumanity to man, and all along the life of the sea and its creatures carries on, foraging for food, eating, swimming, migrating, giving birth. It is a great mystery that gives the heart pause," he thought. "We are but a tiny part of all that unfolds, on this green and hallowed earth." Words from the Bible came to mind: "For behold, the winter is past. The rain is over and gone ... And the voice of the turtle is heard in the land."

He thought about the soldiers in the 54th Regiment still giving their lives for the cause of abolition and equality and still receiving no pay at all to send home to their families. He knew many of them were destitute and felt powerless and defeated. And yet, they persevered. They remained loyally engaged. He shook his head in wonder at their integrity and fortitude. These men were all he wished them to be. Noble servants of the cause. Once back in Massachusetts he would do his part to make right this one wrong he could have a say in. He leaned back on the bench and let the movement of the waves and the sun and sea air gently relax his mind. The ship was accompanied by a flock of sea birds, wheeling across the sky, blocking the sun, moving like a single veil, back across the wake, arcing across the sky and swooping back again. And the wake was like a ribbon of silver winding along behind the ship. Sam's eyes closed and he was asleep.

# Chapter 13

Sam had been home for three weeks. His return had been subdued due to his weakened state. His furlough came to an end. After much discussion with Ellen who had been caring for him, he determined he did not have the stamina to return south. He sent in his resignation as Chaplain, supported by a letter from his personal physician and was granted an honorable discharge by Governor Andrew. He had continued his petitions to the War Office and Governor Andrew had written to President Lincoln on March 24th, 1864, the following:

"*Sir:*

*I beg leave to submit to your consideration by this communication and accompanying papers, the case of Reverend Samuel Harrison, lately Chaplain of the 54th Regiment of Mass. Volunteers.*

*Mr. Harrison was duly elected Chaplain of the 54th Mass. Vol. Infy. on August 22nd 1863; was commissioned by me as such, September 8th, 1863 and was mustered into the service of the United States, Nov. 12th, 1863 at Morris Island, SC by Charles A. Brooks mustering officer.*

*On demanding his pay as Chaplain, of the U.S. Paymaster at Hilton Head, he was met by the following refusal in writing, viz:*

*Hilton Head, S.C. Feb. 6th 1864.*

*Samuel Harrison, Chaplain of the 54th asks pay at the usual rate of $100 per month, and two rations, which, he being of African descent, I decline paying, under Act of Congress passed July 17, 1862 employing persons of African descent in military service of the United States. The Chaplain declines to receive anything less.*

*Signed, A. Ten Eyck, Paymaster U.S.A*

~

The letter, being many, many pages, went on to point out that: *"....The case of Chaplain Harrison however carries us a step further, as it is the case of an officer, duly mustered into the service of the United States, who has performed the duties of an officer and claims the full pay of an officer.*

*More than this, it is the case of a man filling a sacred office, one who has presented the lawful testimonials of the appropriate ecclesiastical authorities, proving that he is a clergyman in good and regular standing with his denomination; one who has been legally elected by the votes of the field officers and company commanders of a volunteer regiment, to the office of Chaplain.... If as a private soldier, he might not have been by reason of his color, entitled to the full pay of a soldier, even while performing the full duty of a soldier; if, as an officer of United States Volunteers, he was, by reason of his color, to be deprived of the compensation provided by law for officers of his rank and grade; yet it will be the first time, I believe, since the Christian era, that a man in holy orders, in the Christian Church has by reason of his color, descent or origin been refused the rights, immunities and privileges pertaining to his office and character ..."*

*I have the honor to be, Your Excellency's Obt. Servant,*

*John A. Andrew*

This letter, endorsed by President Lincoln, was forwarded to the Attorney General, Edward Bates, for his legal opinion as to whether the Pay Master should have paid as demanded and if, whether it is the duty of the President to order him to pay.

Edward Bates did respond, vigorously, that in his opinion Chaplain Samuel Harrison deserved his pay, and that he had not been appointed under the law of July 17, 1862 (which was the grounds upon which the pay had been denied.)

He claimed that:

*"The 54th Massachusetts Regiment was therefore organized and mustered into the service of the United States under clear authority of law ... The closest inspection of these provisions will discover nothing that precludes the appointment of a Christian minister to the office of Chaplain because he is a person of African descent. I therefore conclude that Mr. Harrison was lawfully appointed and qualified Chaplain of the 54th Massachusetts Regiment ... To assume that because Mr. Harrison is a person of African descent, he shall draw only the pay which this law establishes for the class it obviously refers to, and be deprived of the pay which another law specifically affixes to the office he lawfully held, would be, in my opinion, a distortion of both laws, not only unjust to him but in plain violation of the purpose of Congress.*

*I therefore think that the Paymaster should have paid Mr. Harrison his full pay as Chaplain of a volunteer regiment. And, he went on to say:*

"*Your attention having been specifically called to the wrong done in this case, I am also of opinion that your constitutional obligation to take care that the laws be faithfully executed, makes it your duty to direct the Secretary of War to inform the officers of the Pay Department of the Army that such is your view of the law, and I do not doubt that it will be accepted by them as furnishing the correct rule for their action.*

*I am, Sir,*

*Very respectfully, Your obedient Servant,*

*Edward Bates*"

~

Sam carefully re-read his copy of the letter forwarded to him by Governor Andrew. He saw that President Lincoln had received this letter on or about April 23, 1864, and that it clearly stated that he (President Lincoln) had the duty to direct the Secretary of War "*to inform the officers of the Pay Department of the Army that such is your view of the law, and I do not doubt that it will be accepted by them as furnishing the correct rule for their action.*"

~

Sam sighed. He had heard that President Lincoln had not done this. Rather he put it in the hands of Congress to pass a law requiring equal pay for all the properly mustered colored troops. What kind of strategy was this? How long would they have to wait? Congress was not known for fast action. However, it did make the issue more public and that was good.

"I have heard that a few soldiers have been shot dead for not accepting the lower pay rate. Is this true?" asked a young woman of Sam.

Sam and Ellen were outside the church speaking with a group from the congregation gathered to discuss how to distribute food to the families of those Berkshire County men who were fighting in the South and not receiving payment. Many of the families were destitute, not able to find extra work to feed their children.

"What I have heard," said Sam, "is that five soldiers have been shot due to what was described as insubordination. Now this could mean any number of things, one of them being they refused their lower pay."

"Well, what do we do? I hear also that those men who have joined the 54th and 55th after we had lost so many men at Fort Wagner are not very keen to let their families suffer this level of poverty. There is not unity among the soldiers anymore."

"Do we still have enough men willing not only to die for their freedom but also allow their families to perhaps die of starvation for the cause?"

"Well, some of these soldiers are from the South itself and have a different attitude towards the issue," said Sam. "I have heard tell that they say our men at least know where their families are and that they are surrounded by friends. These Southern men, having escaped the plantations to join the Union army, have left their families only to God."

"This is true," said another.

"We are *truly* still not emancipated."

The gathering fell silent.

Sam felt he had to say something to lift the mood. "Faith

is a substance. It is the acceptance of things hoped for and the evidence of things not seen. And we have faith. We are strong in our faith that all will be well. We shall pray for our deliverance. We shall pray for equal pay and justice for our people."

There was a solemn nodding and a few smiles. Hope was what they had.

"We will bring what food and contributions we can tomorrow to the church," said Ellen. "Let's see how many families we can help."

~

For the next few months Sam remained in Pittsfield with his family. His experience in the South had left a deep impression on him. In the parts of the South where the Union army had prevailed, the former slaves, now free, were destitute. Their previous means of support, although untenable, had provided basic housing and a meal a day. Now they had nothing, some only the clothes on their backs. As the Union troops advanced and took possession of the Sea Islands and the key forts along the coast, the freedmen and women followed the army camp helping where they could. The men dug graves, latrines and ditches. The women helped in the mess tents, as cooks preparing meals, and as nurses tending the wounded and making medicine. They did the same work as white men and women, but were being paid at a lower rate than their white cohorts. Sam determined this was another injustice that must be righted. Maybe he could be of help here, as well. He wondered often when Congress would see fit to examine the issue of unequal pay for the soldiers. Perhaps after that he could concentrate on righting other inequities.

"The church is the center of my life but sometimes I feel I

am a voice crying in the wilderness, a lonely soul crying out for the uplift of my people. Here I can speak what is in my heart and my people can hear me. But what of the wider world? What of our representatives in Congress? How do we get it across to them that we are in dire need of their attention, even as we fight this war?"

Sam spoke longingly of a time when there would be resolution for this deeply cruel and willful misreading of constitutional law. If his family in the North was feeling the ill effects of unequal pay which translated into no pay, how must the families of those soldiers still fighting feel?

~

Finally, in July of 1864, eighteen months after the men of the 54th enlisted, Congress passed the necessary law and finally not only Sam but all the colored troops were sent back pay to the time they had enlisted. They had won their case! They could feed their families, hold their heads up with pride. It had been a bitter battle and it had taken a great toll but they had triumphed. "It can be done," said Sam, "We can make our voices heard. But how many families have suffered needlessly because of the lack of concern for our well-being?"

"Dearest! What shall we do with this largesse?" Ellen queried when his scrip had arrived from Washington DC. She smiled happily at him and suggested they spend the day at Pontoosuc Lake and eat ices and swim to their hearts content. It would be a joyous occasion and one they would not soon forget. All that waiting, all that scrimping and saving was, for now, a thing of the past.

# Chapter 14

Now Sam felt he could take the next step on his path of life. He recognized that he could help the war effort the most by returning to work for the National Freedmen's Relief Society. For the rest of the summer and the fall he traveled the length and breadth of Massachusetts soliciting clothing and other donations for the freedmen in the South. Anything that could be transported south would be of help. Primarily he visited the churches and spoke with ministers and congregations. People were generous. He often thought of Mrs. Bewick and Mrs. Wentworth, the two women he had met on the *Fulton* on the trip home. They had been adamant that the need for teachers was paramount. As a result he spoke to the congregations about the need for teachers. Some of the young folk expressed an interest in traveling to the South to help out.

He told Ellen later, having observed that many of the white churches had never heard a Black pastor preach, "They probably never had been addressed by a son of Ham before!" Sam was proud to be a "son of Ham", who was, according to the Book of Genesis, a son of Noah. And the descendants of Noah—Shem, Ham and Japheth—after the flood, peopled the whole earth. The darker races are regarded as the descendants of Ham.

Sam was also determined to make the unequal payment of the freed slaves known to all.

"It is the color of their skin, not their skills, that determine their pay," explained Sam to the women after the service.

"All of them, Black and White, work side by side keeping the camps clean and safe, the soldiers healthy, well fed, and supplied with enough medicine as possible under the circumstances. They work side by side but our people, those of African descent, because of their heritage and despite the reason for this war, receive $7/ month, if anything at all." Sam shook his head in incomprehension. "There is no logic to this, only blatant racism."

His parishioners asked him what could be done.

"Well, I will continue soliciting volunteers to go to the South to help with refugees and freedmen," he suggested. "I suspect almost every family has been torn apart in the chaos of the war. These volunteers can also help separated families reunite with their lost family members. It is a tough assignment but one that can have great rewards, as you can imagine!"

Sam turned his head to one side. His eyes had filled with tears as he saw in his imagination a family reunited after years of war and separation. He surreptitiously wiped his eyes. When he was again composed he continued:

"And we will need teachers to help everyone to learn to read and write. As you know, it has been against the law to teach a slave to read or write. Knowledge is power and ..." Sam's voice drifted off again as he thought of the conditions he had seen in the South: the poverty, the ignorance, the destitution ... And how much still had to be accomplished. He recollected himself when he saw the kind eyes of the women looking inquiringly at him. They appreciated his soft-hearted nature.

"Ah, yes! Well, you, we, will collect whatever goods we can to send south to ensure they at least have clothes to wear and a bit to eat!"

Sam looked around at the baskets of clothing, the bedding and shoes, the bags of flour and potatoes. He knew that this would barely make a dent in the poverty and misery of his people. But it was a start. "You have to begin somewhere, I guess!" he muttered to himself.

"And, we can keep our prayers going for a hasty end to this carnage," he continued. "Money would also be of help. A dollar here, a dollar there will go a long way in securing them something to eat."

The women nodded and after the church service the next day a collection was taken up to send to the Aid Society.

He continued working for the Aid Society throughout the winter and into the spring. He felt better doing practical work to ease the destitution he had seen in the South.

And then the news came. The war between the southern and the northern states had come to an end. The war to free the slaves from bondage, the war to right the egregious wrongs perpetrated against the Black race for economic gain, was over, done, won by those wishing for emancipation, equality and freedom for men and women of African descent. It was over.

Sam and Ellen and their children, young Ellen, Mary, George and Lydia, joined the crowds on the streets of Pittsfield marching down North Street to the beat of drums, the call of the bugles and the shouting of the people in joy and in sorrow. Joy for the freedoms gained and sorrow for the lives lost. *The Battle Cry of Freedom* rang through the streets *"Oh we'll rally round the flag boys, we'll rally once again, shouting the battle cry of freedom! The Union forever, hurrah boys hurrah, down with the traitor and up with the star..."*

Robert E. Lee, the southern general, had surrendered to Ulysses S. Grant at Appomattox Court House in Virginia on April 9, 1865. General Sherman's terrible march to the sea had been successful. Much of the South lay in ruins and there was nothing more to be gained from fighting. Consequently, General Lee surrendered.

The rejoicing, however, was cut short by the news, five days later, of the assassination of their beloved President Lincoln. The news shocked the nation. Now the leader they had looked towards in President Lincoln to guide the process of Reconstruction, and to reunite the country, would be in the hands of the Vice President, Andrew Johnson. The Vice President, a southerner, had far less sympathy for, and dedication to, the complexity of establishing true equality of citizenship, of putting into place the foundational reasons for the war, the abolition of slavery and the establishment of a nation devoted to true equality and liberty for all its citizens, Black or White.

President Lincoln had made a plan for putting the country back together again after the war. Most of the fighting had been in the South and much of the South had to be rebuilt. Also, the Southern States had to agree to make slavery illegal before they could rejoin the Union. Lincoln's plan was to say the Southern States could be readmitted into the Union if 10 percent of its voters supported rejoining. But after his assassination Vice President Johnson became president. His plan was different. Being a southerner himself, he wanted to make it easier for the Confederate States to rejoin the Union. But he had no agreed upon strategy for giving the former slaves citizenship or equal status, or the ability to participate in civil or political life. Consequently, Congress stepped in and passed three new amendments to the United States Constitution: the 13th Amendment which outlawed slavery; the 14th Amendment which gave citizenship to Blacks and equal protection under the law; and the 15th Amendment which gave all men, Black and White, the right to vote, as well as to hold office and participate in political life. Four million people of African descent had been enslaved and now they were free citizens of the United States with no real plan in place to integrate the former slaves into free life, no plan in place to make it possible for the freedmen to earn a living, or have somewhere to live. Many of the former slaves who had just been freed from bondage, had been living on plantations, and now had nowhere to go, no place to live with their re-united families, no place to work, no land to till.

Many of the Union regiments, including the 54th, were kept on as the occupying army in the defeated South, to see to the prisoners of war, to the clean-up of towns, to the rebuilding of bridges and roads, to build schools for the poor and Black children, to work with the citizens to restore the productivity of farms that had been abandoned by their owners when the Union army came through. General Sherman's "march to the sea" had laid a wide swath of destruction that needed to be rebuilt. Many of the freedmen were hired to help with reconstructing the roads and towns and building schools, and as a result, had a way to support their families. But it did not go smoothly. The death of President Lincoln blurred the scope of Reconstruction and there were few people overseeing the whole picture.

Sam, in thinking about the reconstruction of the South had told Ellen: "As in any war there is always a victor and the vanquished. On both sides there are good people, and innocent people caught in the crossfire. And on both sides there are also evil people. I think there are only a few people who are truly evil." He had paused and sighed heavily. "But these people can be effective retarding forces for reconstruction. We must fight this as much as we can by providing opportunities for education and advancement. That is why I am working for the Freedmen's Relief Society."

~

Over the next five years the freedmen, with the help of the occupying Union army, made great strides to learn trades, re-enliven and restore abandoned farms to grow food, to educate themselves and to be a part of the rebuilding of the southern economy. Much land had been confiscated from the southern plantation owners and there had been an expectation and a dream at the end of the war that each newly freed family be presented with "40 acres and a mule" to farm the abandoned or confiscated lands. This, however, did not occur. The plantation owners were outraged at being told what they had to do with their land. There was confusion, disorder and even anarchy as each southern state struggled to recover. And there was almost complete resistance to giving any land to former slaves, no matter that everyone, Black and White, was starving for food and thousands of acres of land lay fallow and uncultivated.

As per President Lincoln's Reconstruction plan, in the first few years after the war, Blacks were elected to public office, including as mayors, governors, and members of Congress and had a true voice in guiding the process of Reconstruction. But there was violent opposition to this by southern governments and the Ku Klux Klan and other groups like it, rose to prominence. The struggle of the Whites to suppress the rights of the Black population grew widespread and violent.

It took five years for all the southern states to rejoin the Union and much prejudice and violence was perpetrated against the newly freed slaves in those years. During that time the southern states tried to get around the laws passed by Congress and the three new Amendments to the Constitution, by enacting Black Codes. These were restrictive codes which made it nearly impossible in some southern states for Blacks to vote, get jobs, support their families, send their children to school, or to own land. The Union army tried to enforce the new Constitutional Amendments that were, in reality, the law of the land put in place to protect the rights of the former slaves. But bigoted southern leaders had other plans in mind.

"You can have a law but if there is no one to enforce it....." Sam fretted, "what good is it? We must, we must, remain committed to enforcing the laws."

But, over time, with so much resistance from the South, the northern states became disillusioned and discouraged. There was little leadership from anyone, and the years after the war were painfully unproductive, violent and chaotic. Finally northern politicians gave up any interest in what happened in the South and withdrew the Union troops and the South was left to its own devices. The loss of President Lincoln was a true tragedy that set the course for the dismal future of race relations in the United States.

Despite the fact that by 1870 more than 1,000 freedmen

schools had been established and the Freedman's Bureau was able to offer limited health care, as well as seeds for farmers and planters to grow food for their families and to sell in the markets, the situation was dire. The white Southerners were opposed to any kind of education for the Blacks. Southern whites had again regained power and they took away many of the education funds, passed Jim Crow* laws, established legal segregation, and continued aggressively preventing Black people from holding office or exercising their rights to citizenship and to vote. The Northerners who had been helping the Freedman's Bureau and the Government to rebuild the South and create jobs, grew weary of the struggle for justice. The violence against the former slaves, the outright hostility and racism were such an enormous force that the North slowly withdrew. They gave up. Racism in the South was deep-seated and systemic as was the fear of retaliation. The people who were helping were ready for the South to take care of itself. Which it did, by creating new constitutions and "separate but equal" laws that segregated Blacks from Whites. It was a terrible time that set a terrible precedent for the centuries that would follow.

---

* *Jim Crow laws legalized segregation between Blacks and Whites*

# Chapter 15

"This is so discouraging, Ellen. I cannot see but that we have come full circle despite the war," Sam said bitterly as the two of them were getting ready to move the family to Newport, Rhode Island, where Sam had been offered a ministry.

"We've made no progress, the condition of our race is as bad as before."

Ellen looked at him, knowing that despite his eagerness to meet new challenges, he was deeply distressed by the news coming from the South.

"Well, could we look at the situation as a spiral rather than a circle?" asked Ellen. "Yes, we appear to have come full circle but we're in a different place. We have traveled from the battlefield, we are "free," we are slaves no more. We have opportunities we didn't have before. Try to look at it as a spiral ever so slowly moving upwards."

Ellen looked inquiringly at Sam. She had confidence in his decision to move to Newport. He had become too despondent focusing primarily on the troubles in the South. To her surprise, he was nodding in agreement. "You're right, Ellen. That is the way to look at it. Even if the landscape looks the same, it has changed. We are slightly better off," said Sam. "I do so appreciate your way of looking at things. Thank you dearheart."

Ellen was relieved to see the cloud lifting from Sam's soul. She knew he was near to exhaustion and really needed to be focusing on his vocation rather than everything else he was doing.

Sam had been criss-crossing Massachusetts for months after the end of the war, petitioning different congregations for any kind of help for the Freedmen's Relief Society. He was determined to do his part to help rebuild the South. He had not been home in weeks and Ellen knew he had not been eating or sleeping well. "Sam, you need to settle down again. All this travel is hard on your body and soul."

"I know it. I know it. It is hard on me but I feel powerless to help and so much is needed to make the situation in the South more bearable. But I'll bear that in mind, dear Ellen."

A week later, during his travels he had met with a minister looking for someone to lead a church in Newport. At one time Rhode Island had been the largest slave trading port in the country. Sam thought about what it would be like to live and work in a place that had contributed so much to the misery of his people and to the situation they were now in, still fighting for their rights as human beings. He contacted the search committee and went for a visit in the last week in July of 1865.

"You come highly recommended to us, Reverend Harrison. We have heard of your eloquent sermons, your strong faith and your consistent uplift of your people. We admire that in a man!" said a member of the search committee.

"Yes, well, I'm well aware of the challenges people of my

race face, even today, after so many years of battle and our emancipation," replied Sam.

"We'd like to hire you forthwith! When can you start?"

"I must consult with my wife, Ellen. But I think she'll be happy with this opportunity."

After speaking with Ellen, Sam had made the arrangements for the family to move that autumn and start his ministry in Newport. He was relieved to be returning to the leadership of a congregation, to nurturing souls, to affairs of the spirit and of God. His family at that point consisted of four children plus his wife and himself. Hester had recently married Richard Laing from Newark, New Jersey and after their wedding, moved with him to New Jersey.

Despite being well received and well liked, Sam was disheartened by the lack of spirituality in the congregation. And his children were very unhappy in Newport. The "colored" school they were to attend had been merged with a "white" school. Each of his children, despite being excellent students, experienced immediate prejudice from the white pupils and their parents. When Mary won the school-wide spelling bee it had enraged the other students so much that they threw spitballs at her and taunted her with racial slurs. That afternoon, upon entering her home she resolved not to return to the school. The school board wrote the Harrisons a letter of apology, begging her to return and promising it would not happen again. Mary was reluctant, but she did finish out the semester.

Depressed about the state of affairs both for his children and for his congregation, Sam sought out another church in Springfield, Massachusetts, where he had had contact during his time working with the Freedmen's Relief Society. It was the church where John Brown, of Harper's Ferry memory, had worshipped with his friends.

"Do you know who John Brown was?" Sam asked his children when telling them about the new church in Springfield.

"I know he was an abolitionist," said Mary, "but not much more."

"Well, he gave his life for the cause of abolition," replied Sam. "Before the war, I think it was in 1859, he and a band of men raided the place where the government stored their guns at Harper's Ferry, Virginia; it's called an arsenal. He thought that by giving weapons to this band of men, both Black and White, they would be able to free many slaves. He was able to capture the weapons but it was a bloody battle and many men were killed. The raid terrified people in Harper's Ferry. They demanded retaliation. There was no Union army at that time, just a U.S. army, and Robert E. Lee was a general in it. He marched to Harper's Ferry with a larger army and took the arsenal back. John Brown was hanged as a traitor." Sam was silent for a moment, looking at the wall above his children's heads. Then he continued. "Despite the fact that John Brown and his men were killed this raid was considered a success.

"Why?" asked Mary.

"Well, because of the country's reaction to it, and the fact that it was so well organized. Both Black and White workers had united together and organized themselves into a unified group of men seeking to change working conditions. It caused the South to recognize that many many people were opposed to slavery in the rest of the country. The South realized it would have to secede from the Union if it wanted to protect its right to own slaves. It became a key event leading to the beginning of the war." Sam finished with a sigh. He knew his history ... but that didn't make it easy to remember.

His children looked at him solemnly. Although they had experienced enough prejudice and racism to know that being Black in America was not easy, they didn't know much at all about what it was like to be a slave. They were glad the war was over.

Sam liked the idea of ministering to a congregation of former abolitionists and his family was glad to leave Newport. Sam was hired immediately. He and his family left for Springfield in December and spent four years there, happily inspiring a sense for the revival of the spirit in his congregation and himself. In Springfield his family encountered less overt discrimination and prejudice, although some was always present.

In the summer of 1870 when Sam was fifty-two years old, he was approached by a church in Portland, Maine to come and be their permanent minister. It was his third call to come to this particular church in Portland, the first having been given eighteen years before in 1852. So many calls from a church was an uncommon occurrence and Sam felt he ought to give it a try. His family was willing, even though his children would have to change schools again. It was a good move. The schools were open to "colored" students and Mary and little Ellen excelled at their high school studies as did George and Lydia in their elementary school classes.

They remained happily in Portland until 1872 when Sam received a letter inviting him to return to his original congregation in Pittsfield. The letter also stated that he would be guaranteed a living wage. He and Ellen discussed the possibility of their return and decided that, despite the disruption of yet another move, the ties they felt to their original community were strong enough to draw them back.

"This'll be our last move, my dear Ellen," Sam promised his wife. "And, we'll find a place for Mary to stay while she finishes out her senior year here."

The family was sitting around the table eating their Sunday dinner. It was late March and the winds still howled around their windows and whistled through the bare branches of the trees on the street. The visible sky was a pale blue and there was no real sign of the sun. Winter in Maine stretched out far into May. Portland was a coastal city and although it was warmer overall than in the Berkshire hills of Massachusetts, because of the ocean the cold of winter seemed to last longer.

"Yes, that's a must," replied Ellen looking at Mary. "We can't ask Mary to leave her friends in the last months of school, can we dear?"

"Oh Father," said Mary, "Thank you!" Mary beamed at her family looking at each face around the table. "Tomorrow after school my friends and I are going to get measured for our class rings. I'm very excited! I may go with them, mayn't I, Father?"

Sam looked at his daughter with great pride. He turned away briefly to brush a tear away on his shirt sleeve. "Dear Mary, of course you can go. I'm so proud of you, you know I am."

"And what about me?" exclaimed little Ellen. "What about my friends? I'm in 10th grade, can't I finish out my school year here?"

"We'll see about that," replied Sam, "I'll be returning next week to Pittsfield to organize getting the house ready for our moving in again. However long that takes will be the deciding factor!"

As Sam traveled back to Pittsfield to meet with the board members of the church he felt as if his journey was not through space but rather through time, the veils of years being drawn back, one by one, for him to look at and take into account who he had been, who he had become and how he had changed. He was glad to be going home. He felt his travelling times were over.

Within a few days he was satisfied that all would be as he had been led to believe. He stayed to get the house and garden ready and within a month the family moved back to Pittsfield.

"No warmer friends have I had anywhere than in Pittsfield," Sam exclaimed as he picked Ellen and the children up at the Pittsfield train station. "This is to be our last move, I can feel it!"

Puffy clouds drifted across the sky as the sun shone warmly on their faces. In the stately elms lining the street a flock of red-winged blackbirds chattered in the branches. He breathed in deeply, content to be back where he had first started as a minister.

"It is here where I feel the strength to take up my next tasks in life," he continued as they wheeled their luggage cart through the streets to their home on Third Street, not far from the station. "It is here where I can carry on my work for the true emancipation of our race."

Ellen nodded, happy to be back where she felt most at home. It had been seven years of zigzagging across New England and it was time to settle again in one place.

That evening, once again within the familiar walls of the house they had built from the ground up, Sam took up the thread of conversation he had greeted them with.

"It is here that I will again take up the pen to fight for racial and social justice, for our people. I will again have time to write! And you all will finish school, and you, dear wife, you can take up your sewing again with your friends!"

Ellen smiled. Sam was fired up and both she and the children were glad to see his eyes ablaze.

Back with his congregation, Sam's sermons were often appeals for the people of Pittsfield to take note of the goings on in the South. He encouraged his parishioners to try and influence Congress to hold to their promises of Reconstruction. News continually trickled in about the terrible state of the nation's freed people in the South. The feeling of powerlessness that Sam often felt was ameliorated by the fact that he had his pulpit. It was there, during the week, and twice on a Sunday, that he could give vent to his frustrations about the slow pace of progress towards equality in the South.

"We can't look towards the white men in power to make sure that every day the Nation is brought a step closer to racial, social and economic justice. We must contribute if there is to be progress," he said from the pulpit. "If we don't take an active part we cannot criticize. And, to be honest, if we follow the goings-ons in the South we see actual regression. This is not an illusion! This is unacceptable! In the first years after the war we had the right to *vote*. We held *political office,* we were *members of Congress, governors, mayors.* Our right to vote was used well. A majority of us in the South used our heads and hands to further our progress. It appeared that great strides were being taken to exercise our newly recognized citizenship. We, former slaves, helped set up schools in villages and towns, and we taught many children who were eager to learn how to read and write. Some Confederate lands were confiscated for the establishment of schools. The adults, also, studied reading and writing. We knew full well that education was our key to true freedom. But there's much southern resistance and bigotry. I fear we're losing ground despite our emancipation and our efforts."

Sam continued in this vein Sunday after Sunday. He wanted his people to write letters to the editors of southern newspapers, to write to their representatives to urge them to stay active in the reconstruction of the South, to make the southern states stick to President Lincoln's original plan.

"I just cannot see us giving up now," he said to Ellen. "As you remind me, it is a spiral. We *are* getting *somewhere* even if we can't see it. But we can't stop our vigilance. I'm afraid that if we do, our road to racial integration will be longer and harder than can be imagined."

# Chapter 16

In 1874 Sam was asked to write a retrospective of the city of Pittsfield, which he did. *Pittsfield Twenty Five Years Ago* became a labor of love. It was an opportunity to get to know his adopted hometown from an historical perspective and he became more well-known to all the citizens of Pittsfield. It was well appreciated and helped to keep his mind off the situation in the South.

§§§

Twelve years had passed since the end of the war and Sam had been busy with his church, writing sermons, holding revivals, visiting families, comforting the sick, easing peoples' grief at the loss of a family member, making sure each family had enough to eat despite the hard times. To commemorate the celebration of 100 years since the Declaration of Independence he had written a Centennial pamphlet to the citizens of Berkshire County: "Shall a Nation be born at once? A Centennial Sermon." It had sold over 500 copies.

His focus on writing had helped him bear the death of their daughter Mary who had died suddenly of pneumonia in 1875, sending both of them into a grief so deep they thought they would not recover. She was twenty years old. This time Ellen seemed to take longer to pull through. She had depended so much on Mary for moral and emotional support.

"My heart is sore. My mind cannot take this in," she wept to Sam. "How can I go on without her?"

Sam was at a loss. But he held her, nursed her daily as she lay pallidly in her bed. One day he told her,

"Hester is coming for a visit."

"How can she leave her family?" Ellen asked distractedly.

"She is bringing them with her. Little Sam and Laura-Grace and your namesake Ellen!"

"Oh my!" Ellen perked up. "They are coming here? All that way? Then, I must get up and prepare."

"Oh no you don't! They're all coming to help take care of you!"

"But we will need things to eat!" she cried. "I haven't baked in weeks."

"I have asked your sewing group to help me prepare for their visit. They will be here shortly. You are to rest." Sam was firm and Ellen, with the love of her family, was able to get back on her feet.

~

Two years later, in 1879, the congregation had shrunk again. Many families had been moving from Pittsfield to find work elsewhere. Sam was concerned about the dismal working conditions for Blacks in the North. He had been researching employment opportunities all summer for many of the men of the 54th. They had returned from the South eager to take up their lives again. But there was no work. The factories and mills were not hiring Black men, despite their war record and experience rebuilding the South and holding positions of authority. It was debilitating and his research showed an engrained racism that he had not heretofore been that aware of. His lack of success had begun to wear at his gut. Ellen recognized the signs of impending distress.

"Why don't you undertake another writing project, Sam?" Ellen queried. "You could write it for a wider audience than Pittsfield."

Sam didn't answer.

"Sam, my dear husband!" she placed a hand on his shoulder knowing there was not much she could do to help. "I shall make us a cup of tea. Lydia and George will be home soon and we will set about preparing the garden. Then we will have your favorite stew for supper." Ellen knew this was a weak antidote to Sam's gloom but she also knew that daily routine could help ease Sam's melancholy.

Sam knew what Ellen was doing and lifted his head to smile wanly at her. He knew she was right. He would have to do something creative, something useful for the country, something that might affect the state of people's minds.

After supper that evening Sam sat down at his desk. He would address this treatise to his own people as well as the rest of the citizens of the United States. He would write this for publication.

Over the next few months, alongside his ministerial duties Sam wrote *"An Appeal of a Colored Man to his Fellow Citizens of a Fairer Hue, in the United States."*

*This appeal is addressed to my fellow-citizens of the United States, because the subject matter of the appeal directly concerns them; for nowhere else in the world is such an appeal necessary. The conventional rules of society are nowhere else so rigid as in the United States of*

America. Color here is a barrier to every calling, except the most menial and humble. Hence we appeal to those who can correct, or at least help to correct, the matter of which we complain, and thus bring about results which will be advantageous to those to whom I address myself, as well as for those for whom this appeal is made. It is a fact that cannot be ignored, however much men may be disposed to, that the colored man labors under difficulties and burdens which no other people do. It is true that he has been emancipated. It is true that he has been enfranchised. The one was the result of military necessity, unavoidably. The other was the needs of the government to help maintain its power over the disloyal States. Had the government at the same time given the emancipated and enfranchised Freeman of the South confiscated land, or appropriated land from the public domain, for their occupancy, it would have been one of the wisest measures accomplished. And it would have helped them, and also have saved the government much of the trouble which since their emancipation has been brought about, and will in all probability continue until some such measure is accomplished.

Nowhere have an emancipated people been sent out so empty-handed as the freed people of the South. Their disloyal owners hold the land. The wealth which the rebels hold today is from the unrequited toil of the ex-slaves; and if the freed people of the South had their dues they would be the owners of every foot of land in the Southern States. All the wealth of the South belongs to them really and truly; for the very year that the May Flower landed the Puritans upon Plymouth Rock, that same year a cargo of *slaves was landed at Jamestown, Virginia, which is over 250 years ago. All these long years they have toiled for the benefit of others, and when emancipated, not a foot of land was donated to them that they might call their own, and even intelligence, and the sources from which intelligence comes are denied them, and even in some places of the South schools which were built by Northern charity for them have been destroyed by the torch of the incendiary. The old hate of the past in relation to the education of the colored man of the South, is today shown in no small degree ...*

~

Sam wrote of the myriad examples of former slaves, freedmen, as well as northern citizens who had been born free who had risen to the top of their profession—doctors, lawyers, congressmen, university scholars, professors who disproved the Southern notion that Blacks were in some way inferior. He ended on a hopeful note, addressing the issue of inequity head on:

*"This has been exemplified upon all occasions when the note of war has been sounded in our land, whether of a domestic or of a foreign character, and most notable in our late Civil War. The greatest pressure to which our government had ever been subjected, after months of conflict between the North and the South, with no decisive results on either side, the colored man was called to arms. And with a degree of courage only equaled by his white brother, he went forth under more discouraging circumstances, because defeat to the Union arms and the triumph of rebellion would have been the signal for the immolation of three millions of human beings, or that*

system which would have been worse to him than death; a more cruel bondage, because thousands have been murdered since, though the rebellion was put down.... Now these colored men were aware of what would have been their fate if God had not been with the Union army— death to them and perpetual slavery, if possible, to their wives and children. But they, with white men, went forth from their homes, with courageous hearts and stalwart arms to meet the issue upon a hundred battlefields. And by the effort of both black and white men, the country was saved from division. The bond of union has been cemented by the blood of white and colored men flowing in one common pool, they are morally obligated to uphold the flag which waved over both in battle and in the throes of death. It is the sign of protection to both, for both have borne it amid the fire and smoke of the battlefield. Both alike have been wrapped in its fold when lying dead. Then by the memories of the battlefields and groan of the dying, and the graves of the dead, I ask my fellow citizens to accord to us that which we have won. See that you do your part in this matter. Let justice stand out in all your acts and dealing towards us; and as we have been true and faithful in the past, under unfavorable circumstances, let the past be a pledge of the future in regard to the race I represent. Justice being done to all classes and conditions, then will our country march on to greatness and glory; more so, in all probability than all the nations of the past. And when the roll of the nations shall be called in the grand consummation, America, perhaps the last, but not the least in the nobleness of her mission and destiny."

Sam put his pen down. He was finished. This piece of work,

this "project" as Ellen liked to call it, was done. He sighed. "No one can hand you your future," he said to himself. "They can only show you the road." And this was his mapping of the road. He could show it. Others could follow it. They must take it. The future of his race, he knew, hung in the balance.

One thousand copies were printed and distributed. Word got around and Mark Hopkins, president of Williams College in nearby Williamstown stopped by for a visit.

"I remember well your speech on "The Cause and Cure for the War" in the beginning of our own civil war. This booklet has the same feel," said Mr. Hopkins.

They were sitting in the parlor, at the front of the house. Sam was fiddling with a cup of tea, vigorously and thoughtlessly stirring in the sugar, while Ellen watched him with concern. Sam did not relish attention, no matter what kind, being showered upon him. Although he and Mr. Hopkins had been friends for over twenty-five years he still looked up to him as the more learned.

"Ah, yes! That talk that I gave in 1862, wasn't it?" he looked at Ellen for confirmation. She patted his hand and nodded.

"Well, those were very confusing times. Did we want a war?" Sam continued. "Did we need one? Was the South truly unconcerned about the moral stain of slavery? Were they so imperceptive to the higher law that recognized the humanity of people of African descent?"

He stopped abruptly. The memory of that time burst vividly into Sam's mind. He remembered the confusion, the inability to know whether to rejoice or mourn when the first shots were fired off the coast of Charleston, South Carolina, those many years ago. "And what have we achieved since the war?"

Mr. Hopkins was looking at Sam with admiration. Sam's passion and loyalty to the fight for justice was clear in his voice and words. "This is just what I came here about, Rev. Harrison!" he said. "We would like you to come to Williamstown to give a talk and then perhaps prepare a series of talks around the state. We see you as an effective motivational speaker."

Sam looked doubtful.

"We need people like you! People who have passion and are articulate and up to date on the politics of the time! It's not going well in the South, as you know. We seem to be regressing to a time worse than before the war. We in the North have abandoned the South. But they need us still. They need our help, our funds, our presence. And this can only happen if the citizens of the northern States are aware of what is going on. You can motivate them!"

Sam began nodding his head in agreement. It seemed like a good idea. He knew he enjoyed speaking to large groups of people. He was passionate about the issues affecting his race. He did hear from his friend, Colonel Higginson about the rise of the Ku Klux Klan, the violence, the lynchings, the Black Codes, the rewriting of State law to prevent the freedmen from voting. Yes, he was well aware of the temper of the South. He looked over at Ellen and remembered her telling him that keeping active is what helped him stay away from the trough of despair. He looked over at his visitor. "I would be delighted to work with you, Mr. Hopkins," said Sam.

Ellen looked up in surprise. She was pleased that the battle she had seen going on in Sam's mind had been won by the forces of light.

"That is just what I had hoped!" said Mr. Hopkins.

The rest of the conversation was about dates and places.

Sam rode the crest of enthusiasm and felt confident that he was up to the task.

Over the next year or so Sam gave a number of rousing talks around the State. He felt a renewed sense of optimism that changes were coming to how the people of his race were regarded and treated. Ellen missed him sorely when he had to be away and he missed being home. The power of the word had always been his strength and it still felt good to speak to an audience and feel their response.

However, in March of 1881, their daughter, Ellen, died at the age of twenty-nine. It was a blow that no one was able to recover from. Sam was heartbroken and he and his wife pulled back from public activities. The next year, in September of 1882, Hester Jane died of a fever at the age of thirty-nine, leaving behind four children. George and Lydia stayed on to help their parents bear their loss.

Then, two years later on Christmas Eve of 1883, his own wife, his dear, dear Ellen, his helpmeet on the path of life, passed away. Her illness had been quick and there was barely anytime to prepare inwardly for the gaping hole this would leave in his life. The family gathered together at the house on Third Street for the unhappiest Christmas in memory. It was hard to imagine the house without her warmth of heart, her positivity, her caring hands and graceful ways.

For the next years Sam tended to his congregation, worked a bit on the shoe bench, visited with his colleagues and friends, played with his grandchildren, and sold more of his books, including the well-received *Centennial Discourse.*

In 1899, when he was 81, he was asked to write his autobiography, which he did, calling it:

*Reverend Samuel Harrison, His Life Story, told by Himself.*

He thought about the trajectory his life had taken, with Ellen at his side for most of the journey. How she had raised his spirits every time he faltered. How she had kept his home, his children, his hearth, warm and safe all those years. Put up with his many absences, his moods, his anguishes. She had shared it all with a grace and love that outshone anything else in his life. True, he had given her the family and home she had dreamed of, but they had done this together. The other things in his life, he realized, were utterly contingent on her presence. What would he have come to without her? Although his autobiographical narrative did not always reflect that she was behind everything he did, he knew, and his children knew, and he thought, most people know that one never accomplishes anything alone.

He died the next year on August 11, 1900, at the age of eighty-two in his home in Pittsfield. His passing was marked by many newspaper articles and commemorations. He was survived by his two remaining children, George Briggs Harrison and Lydia Ann Harrison-Jacobs and four grandchildren: Florence Lewis Jacobs, Harrison D. Jacobs, Maitland Jacobs and Bessie Jacobs. (The children of Hester Jane Harrison Laing are: Samuel S. Laing, Laura Grace Lang Salters, Ellen R. Laing, William Laing, about whom we know very little. Only Laura is known to have survived to adulthood.)

The Reverend Samuel Harrison's
Memorial Tablet read as follows:

## _Samuel Harrison Memorial Tablet_

In Memory of the
Reverend Samuel Harrison,
1818-1900.
Ordained and settled over this
Church as its First Minister, 1850-
62. Again its minister from 1872
until his death in 1900. Member of
the Association of Congregational
Ministers of Berkshire County
for Forty Years. Chaplain 54th
Massachusetts Voluntary Infantry,
1862-3. A Wise Leader, an
Honored Citizen, and Ardent
Patriot, a beloved Messenger of
the Lord, he wrought well for his
People, his Country and his God.
"I have Fought a good Fight. I
have finished my Course, I have
kept the Faith. Henceforth, there is
laid up for me a
Crown of Righteousness."

*Augustus St. Gaudens Memorial to the 54th*
*in Boston, Massachusetts*

# Acknowledgments

The Massachusetts Cultural Council's Local Cultural Councils: Pittsfield, Sheffield, Alford/Egremont, Mt. Washington, Stockbridge, Great Barrington, Monterey, New Marlborough, Lee and Lenox all contributed significantly to making this book possible. Their generosity of spirit, as well, when I had to ask for an extension due to my parents' illness, was vital in paving the way for finishing this book. I thank you all for your faith in me and the process.

Blayne Whitfield, great-great-grandson of Samuel Harrison, who provided me with missing information, context and permission to use whatever he had about his ancestor, including the photographs of young Samuel, and Samuel and Ellen; and Ruth Edmonds Hill, great granddaughter who read the manuscript with an editors eye, I thank you both for your encouragement and support. Frances Jones-Sneed, professor of History at Massachusetts College of Liberal Arts, I thank you for giving me the idea to write this book and for your brilliant designs for the "We the People" NEH grants "*The Shaping Role of Place in African American Biography*" and "*Of Migrations and Renaissances: Harlem and Chicago, 1915-1975*" that introduced me to Samuel Harrison as well as other African American historic figures of Berkshire County,

MA about whom I plan to write, as well. You set the course of my life until these five books are written.

And Dianna Downing for her excellent editing and proof-reading skills and kind words of encouragement. And special thanks go to my readers who waded through this manuscript to give me valuable advice on how to make an historical biography accessible: Jonathan Barnes, Sherry Fichtner, Jana Laiz, Robert Pellaciotti, Richard Meyers, Anna Claire Novotny, Wende Ractliffe and Signe Schaefer.

And as I will for every book that comes through my being, I thank my husband, Richard of twenty plus years for all of his care and inspiration. I truly could not have done this without you.

massculturalcouncil.org

# Authors Note

This book has been forming in my mind since 2006 when I participated in a National Endowment for the Humanities grant *"The Shaping Role of Place in African American Biography"* created and submitted by Frances Jones-Sneed, professor of history at Massachusetts College of Liberal Arts (MCLA.) That is where I was first introduced to five African American historic figures of Berkshire County, Massachusetts, where I live. At that time only Elizabeth "Mumbet" Freeman, was known to me. The other four: Agrippa Hull, Samuel Harrison, James Van der Zee and W.E.B. Du Bois were basically just names I was hearing for the first time. As the months of the grant progressed I realized that these five people needed their stories told, their lives given voice. I felt compelled to write about each of them. As is often the case, life got in the way of beginning the process.

The book about Mumbet *"A Free Woman On God's Earth" The True Story of Elizabeth "Mumbet" Freeman, The Slave Who Won Her Freedom* is the first book, co-authored with Jana Laiz, and now this is the second.

Writing about Reverend Harrison has been a profoundly moving project. To become acquainted with a person through his own autobiography as well as his other body of works is to immerse oneself in a time and place and to live there so completely that conversations between the characters in the book flow naturally onto the page. And through this immersion becoming more aware of the systemic nature of racism in America and all that a person of color has had to contend with since the beginning of our country has made a deep and abiding change in my life. Coupled with coming to know some of the active personalities peopling the main stage of the 19th Century after having thought I could never penetrate so many different events, has been a gift from the universe. For this I am eternally grateful. I do not in any way maintain that I know what it is like to live as a person of color in this country but I have had a glimpse of so much that needs to change.

## Samuel Harrison's House Today

# BIBLIOGRAPHY

REV. SAMUEL HARRISON—His Life Story—As Told by Himself, Pittsfield, Massachusetts, published at the behest of New York University

AN APPEAL OF A COLORED MAN, to his Fellow-Citizens of a Fairer Hue, in the United States, Rev. Samuel Harrison, Pittsfield, Mass. Chickering & Axtell, Steam Book and Job Printers 1877

CENTENNIAL SERMON: "Shall a Nation be Born at Once?" by Rev. Samuel Harrison, Delivered July 2, 1876

REVEREND SAMUEL HARRISON: A Nineteenth Century Black Clergyman, Dennis Dickerson, in Black Apostles at Home and Abroad: Afro-Americans and the Christian Mission from the Revolution to Reconstruction, edited by David W. Wills and Richard Newman (Boston: G.K. Hall & Co., 1982).

Personal correspondence Blayne Whitfield, great-great grandson of Samuel Harrison

Berkshire Evening Eagle, (Berkshire Athenaeum Local History Files)

Chaplain's Call To Glory Began At WRA, Story of Rev. Samuel Harrison at Western Reserve Academy; Thomas L. Vince, archivist, "News of the Old Reserve," Fall 2002, Western Reserve Academy, Hudson, Ohio

*Colonel Thomas Wentworth Higginson*, article by
Casey Pellerin and Noah Sheola, Boston Athenaeum,
November 2011

*How Slavery Really Ended In America*
Adam Goodheart April 1, 2011 New York Times Magazine

The 54th Massachusetts Regiment History Engine, Tools for
Collaborative Education https://historyengine.richmond.edu/

*Abraham Lincoln Papers at the Library of Congress:*
John A. Andrew to Abraham Lincoln, Thursday, March 24,
1864 *(Equal pay for Samuel Harrison)*
Edward Bates to Abraham Lincoln, Saturday, April 23, 1864
*(Case of Samuel Harrison)*
Senate, Saturday, April 30, 1864, Senate Resolution
John A. Andrew to Abraham Lincoln, Friday, May 13, 1864
*(Case of Samuel Harrison)*

A BRAVE BLACK REGIMENT, The Entire History of
the 54th Massachusetts, 1863-1865, Luis F. Emilio, De Capo
Press, New York, (an unabridged re-publication of 1894 edition)

BATTLE CRY OF FREEDOM, The Civil War Era;
James McPherson, Oxford University Press, 1988

VOICES OF A PEOPLE'S HISTORY of the United
States; Howard Zinn, Anthony Arnove, A Seven Stories
Press First Edition, New York, 2004

BEEN IN THE STORM SO LONG, The Aftermath of Slavery; Leon F. Litwack; First Vintage Books Edition, August 1980, originally published by Alfred A. Knopf, Inc., New York 1979

REMINISCENCES OF MY LIFE IN CAMP with the 33d United States Colored Troops Late 1st S.C. Volunteers: Taylor, Susie King, b. 1848, Electronic Edition.

UNEQUAL FREEDOM, How Race and Gender Shaped American Citizenship and Labor; Evelyn Nakano Glenn, 2002 First Harvard University Press

TWO NATIONS, Black and White, Separate, Hostile and Unequal; Andrew Hacker; Charles Scribner's Sons, NY, 1992, Macmillan Publishing Company NY

NARRATIVE OF THE LIFE OF FREDERICK DOUGLASS, an American Slave—by Himself Frederick Douglass, The Anti-Slavery Office 1845

THE REPUBLIC OF SUFFERING, Death and the American Civil War, Drew Gilpin Faust, 2008 Vintage Books, Random House, Inc., New York

THE PROBLEM OF EMANCIPATION, The Caribbean Roots of the American Civil War; Edward Bartlett Rugemer, Louisiana State University Press, 2008

AMERICAN COLONIES The Settling of North America; Alan Taylor, 2001 Penguin Books USA, 375 Hudson Street, New York, NY 10014

Chief Justice Roger B. Taney Rules against Dred Scott
(1857)

Websites

Samuel Harrison Society, www.samuelharrisonsociety.org

Exploring Diversity in Pennsylvania Ethnic History—www.
hsp.org

Massachusetts 54th Regiment, Massachusetts Historical
Society, MassHist.org

Swamp Angels, a Biographical Study of the 54th
Massachusetts Regiment, True Facts about the Black
Defenders of the Civil War, Robert Ewell Greene
BoMark/Greene Publishing Group, 1990
http://www.latinamericanstudies.org/civil-war/Swamp-Angels.
pdf Robt. Ewell Greene

Mass Moments: www.massmoments.org
August 11, 1841: Frederick Douglass First Addresses a
White Audience
March 12, 1857: John Brown Speaks in Concord
May 28th 1863: 54th Massachusetts Regiment Marches
Through Boston
February 15, 1851: Shadrach Minkins Seized
January 21, 1861: First Militia in MA

Image of Sergeant Wm. Carney from:
http://www.blackpast.org/aah/carney-william-h-1840-1908 (in
public domain)